MOUNT HOLYOKE SEMINARY.
SOUTH HADLEY, MASS.

RECOLLECTIONS OF MARY LYON,

WITH SELECTIONS FROM

HER INSTRUCTIONS TO THE PUPILS

IN

MT. HOLYOKE FEMALE SEMINARY.

BY FIDELIA FISK.

PUBLISHED BY THE
AMERICAN TRACT SOCIETY,
28 CORNHILL, BOSTON.

ROCKWELL AND ROLLINS,
PRINTERS AND STEREOTYPERS,
122 Washington St., Boston.

PREFACE.

The present work is not a memoir. Two considerable volumes have already been published sketching the life and labors of Mary Lyon, and leaving little room or occasion for a third covering the same ground.

Miss Fisk was led to undertake this work by finding among some of the early Holyoke pupils many notes of Miss Lyon's instructions, especially on religious topics, and as these were talked over and interesting incidents were related of her, the desire was very often expressed that they might be put together in some form to benefit others, and bring Miss Lyon anew before the minds of young ladies preparing for usefulness.

Miss Fisk was peculiarly fitted for the work. Her mind and character were of such a type as to receive a deep impress from Miss Lyon's influence. Her birthplace was in a town adjoining Miss Lyon's first home, and, from early childhood, she had heard of her words and deeds. In later years she was brought into intimate connection with her as a pupil and teacher, and allowed, as few others were, to know her inner life. She most tenderly loved and venerated her, and when Miss Fisk went to a distant field of labor, it was to carry Miss Lyon's views and principles with her, and make them pre-eminently her own.

She treasured up every thing she had heard from her lips, and, in studying and following her example, her character was fashioned into the same image. Her instructions to the pupils at South Hadley showed, to all who heard them, that she was imbued with the spirit of their first principal in a remarkable degree.

She entered upon the task of collecting and writing out these reminiscences with much interest, and had nearly completed the narrative portion. It was her purpose to insert only those things which had not been published before; but a few letters and other extracts were desirable to make the narrative complete.

Materials accumulated so much while she was writing that she changed her plan, and designed to re-write much of what she had prepared. Sickness however compelled her to lay aside her pen before she had carried out her purpose, and, after her death, it was thought best to publish the manuscript much as she had left it. It has been copied and finished by a friend, who was a teacher with Miss Fisk at the seminary, and who remained there till after Miss Lyon's death.

This book occupied many of Miss Fisk's thoughts, after disease had laid its hand heavily upon her, and may, perhaps, be considered her last gift to the service of Christ. It was one of the last efforts to be given up. She says of it in speaking of her health, and not being able to return to Persia, —

"I have nothing that I wanted to do here, except to finish that writing. I may have to give it up, but I still hope not. If the tabernacle does not shake too much, I will try to do it, and may be I shall be more in sympathy with her who has laid aside her tabernacle, than if I were well." The book would have had much more merit had she been able to finish it, but the endeavor has been to carry out her wishes and designs in regard to it, as far as possible.

If this record of the instructions and incidents in the life of a beloved teacher shall make her words come home to the heart of any of her pupils with fresh power, and thus incite them to greater diligence in the Master's service, or if it shall give those just commencing life's work new and more correct views of life and duty, the earnest desires of those who have prepared it will be met.

CONTENTS.

SELECTIONS.

RECOLLECTIONS OF MARY LYON.

CHAPTER I.

Parentage and Childhood.

THE OLD MANUSCRIPT — JEMIMA SHEPARD — HER SPIRITUAL CONFLICT — MENTAL ANGUISH — RELIEF — PEACE — LOVE TO CHRIST — ASPIRATIONS — MARRIAGE TO AARON LYON — HIS CONVERSION — BIRTH OF MARY — DEATH OF HER LITTLE BROTHER — AND OF HER FATHER — THE PARTING SCENE — THE WIDOW'S GRIEF — AND JOYS.

"I AM MORE INDEBTED TO MY MOTHER THAN TO ALL OTHERS EXCEPT MY MAKER." — *Mary Lyon.*

WE have recently found an old family register, in which is the following entry: "Jemima Shepard, born January 25th, 1765." When this record was found, there lay close by it a little manuscript book, with a coarse brown paper cover, so unlike any thing of the present day, that it might be supposed to have had its origin in the 17th century. On opening the book, we find that it was written by this same Jemima, in her words, "for her own meditation." It carried us back to the time, when, at the age of fourteen, she opens before us her home among the hills of Western Massachusetts, and an evening hour when she is watching for the return of her parents from a neighboring meeting. She says: "They came, telling me that the minister preached very powerfully, that some were struck under concern, and in particular one of my mates." She adds: "This was the first thing that fastened with any weight on my mind. I thought she was going to be taken and I left. I knew that I stood in as much need of a Saviour as she did; but how I should find him, I could not tell." She was shown how to find him; but not till she had seen what an evil and bitter thing is the sin from which he saved. "Trying to pray," she says, "God appeared to me an angry and frowning judge." She found no fault with this, but adds: "I saw myself justly condemned by his holy and righteous law." She realized that the Spirit of God was striving with her, and the trembling child feared lest she should grieve him; for she says: "I saw that I was entirely helpless without the Spirit of God." But she was to see still more of her heart. In the silent hour of a night when she was alone with God, she says: "It appeared to me that Christ was offered to me, if I was only willing to accept him upon the terms of the gospel. Then I looked into my heart and said to myself, Are you willing to forsake sin and vanity, and all the pleasures of time and sense, and accept of Christ as he is offered to you? Then my stubborn heart replied, I am not willing. I saw my dreadful, stubborn will against God, and that it was as much impossible for me to bow my will as to create a world. I cried out: 'Lord, bow my stubborn will.' I had not a word to say if God should cast me off for ever; for Jesus was offered to me, and I would not accept." She saw herself an enemy to God and all that was good, and with no power to help herself out of this condition. She continued to cry unto God for mercy, and with such a view of her guilt, that she says: "There was no strength left in me." "Totally lost, totally lost," was all that she could say of herself as she sought her chamber one day, after weeks of anguish. She lay before her God, "totally lost." And "there," she says, "my load of guilt was removed, — my stubborn will bowed. I breathed in a new air, and the very first breath was love to God and holiness. I could not bear to sin any more, and I felt my soul drawn out in love to holiness, because God is holy, and to love God, because he is just such a God as he is." For about a week she delighted herself in a holy God, when there came a season of deep distress and darkness. She had not as yet fully learned the way to her Saviour. Jesus had not been clearly revealed to her; but he knew her as his own; and there was given to her, to use her own words, "a longing after Christ," and she was "willing to receive him as Prophet, Priest, and King."

She now delighted herself particularly in the text, "Go ye into all the world, and preach the gospel to every creature;" and says of it: "I stood amazed to think the gospel was preached to me, whom I viewed to be the vilest of Adam's race. But why not be preached to all the rest, and I left out? I thought it would be so just. I viewed myself so vile. But here it was, — 'to *every* creature,' — and therefore to me. Oh, wonder of wonders! I felt my soul drawn out in love to this glorious Saviour, who had died to save the vilest of sinners. I wanted to praise him for ever and ever."

Such was the work of conviction, and such the entrance of light into the heart of this young girl, whom God had chosen, and was now preparing to be the mother of Mary Lyon. As she went on in the Christian life, she makes this record of herself: "Those that I thought loved Jesus appeared to me very lovely and beautiful. I thought they were the only excellent ones of the earth, in whom was all my delight; and when I heard the word preached, my soul would feed thereon." She adds, in charming simplicity: "I had many gracious visits from my blessed and glorious Redeemer. The word of God appeared very precious to me, and many times opened with abundance of clearness to my mind. The cry of my soul was, Lord, what wilt thou have me to do?"

The soul commencing the Christian life, loving God because "he is what he is," and going on with his word opening with "abundance of clearness," while the Saviour's "gracious visits" are "many," is always allowed to glorify that Saviour on earth. And when that soul comes to the close of life, the Father will not chide if its Redeemer's words are made its own: "I have finished the work which thou gavest me to do."

When nineteen years of age, Jemima Shepard became the wife of Aaron Lyon. He seems to have very closely resembled the young man in the gospel. And if he said not "What lack I yet?" others said it of him. The young girl, like her divine Master, "beholding him, loved him;" but she said to him, "One thing thou lackest." Love never blinded her to the fact that "one thing" was wanting.

Her own simple record of her feelings is: "I had a great desire for my companion, that he might believe in Christ, partake of the gospel feast, and travel with me on my heavenly journey."

When she first saw him interested in the subject of religion, she adds: "I was in great distress about him.

I was afraid that his convictions would wear off without *sound* conversion." It was *sound* conversion, no other, that she desired, and for this she prayed most earnestly. But, before it was granted, she was led to say: "I felt willing to *wait* upon God;" and her experience was just that of all God's waiting ones, for she says: "It was not long before the Lord wrought wonders and brought him out of darkness into his marvelous light, and fulfilled all my every desire. When I saw the glory shine into his soul, and saw him so filled with the love of God that he could not forbear crying out, 'Glory to God,' and praising him with all his might, I felt myself, as it were, shrink into nothing before the Lord. I viewed the mercy so great, which I had received, that I wanted to call upon the angels to praise God for me, for I thought myself utterly unworthy to attempt the glorious work while here in the body. But I could not help lisping forth some broken accents of praise to God for his wonderful condescension to me, a poor, unworthy, nothing creature."

And now they could walk *together* in all the commandments of the Lord blameless, and they were rich in faith and good works.

It was to such parents that Mary Lyon was given, in 1797. That was a year of rich spiritual blessing to the little community among whom they resided.

As that mother folds her precious child in her arms

she says: "I hear the birds of Paradise on the boughs of free grace, singing redeeming love. My soul can join in the blessed song, and I rejoice to see the work of the Lord prosper in the hands of the glorious Redeemer."

So she, who was to labor so long and so faithfully in revivals, began her existence where God was pouring out his Spirit, and she was, as it were, prayed into the work by those believing parents.

For nineteen years Aaron and Jemima Lyon walked together on earth, and fifteen of those years they were "one in Christ." Eight children were given them, all of whom were consecrated to the Lord, while one, whom Jesus asked to be with him, became the "family treasure in heaven." "Little Ezra" had been in the Saviour's arms six months, when Mary was welcomed to the mountain home, as she expressed it, "to feel in that family circle the sweetly chastening influence of a babe in heaven." She ever carried this with her, as well as the influence of another scene "where there were sorrowing hearts, bursting sighs, and flowing tears," because death had come to the same house "to take away that affectionate husband, that kindest of fathers." The mother's manuscript tells us how he said in his last days: "Oh, lay me near my Ezra to sleep! Oh, that I had strength to tell you what the Lord has done for me!"

And her own words shall give us the account of his last Sunday morning, while we remember that Mary, then the child of six years, quietly lingered, not only to hear and treasure every word, but to receive an impression upon her young heart that she was to give to many others.

The mother writes: "He said to me, 'I want you to forgive me whatever you have seen in me that was wrong, for I know that I have done wrong a great many times.' I said, 'I think I have more need to ask your forgiveness than you mine, for I think I have been most out of the way.' 'Oh!' said he, 'I can freely forgive you, I have nothing against you.' I said, 'I have nothing against you; I can freely forgive you, and I hope the Lord will forgive us both; and I hope you will recover, and that we shall walk together as heirs of the grace of life, that our prayers be not hindered.' He said: 'Oh, I don't know about that! I wish I had talked more to you when I could. But you must not be too much cast down.'"

During all that day, his feelings were expressed in his own words: "Let me rise upon the mount and wing away."

Monday, the last day of his life, was, in the words of his widow, passed in speaking in holy ejaculations to God, in words like these: "Thou art my rock and my fortress, my high tower and my deliverer. — The name of Christ is as ointment poured forth. — Virgin souls love thee. — Lord Jesus, come quickly."

Tuesday morning, the watching mother brought the seven children to their dying father. The little one of sixteen months in the sister's arms added tenderness to the scene, for in plaintive tones she would say, "Papa, papa," while he blessed them and bade them

"Closer draw that gentle chain
Round the loved who yet remain."

They stand in weeping silence to see their mother draw close to their father's side, and to hear her say: "Are you willing to go and leave me to pass through the troubles and trials alone?" An answer is heard in the father's tender question: "Do you feel your cords long enough and strong enough to wade through the river alone?" She and they heard his last words, and felt that he had gone to be with Christ. They entered "December 21st, 1802," in the old family Bible, as a never-to-be-forgotten day.

The mother says: "I was constrained to say Amen to the will of God, though my nature struggled hard; I seemed to but just survive the shock." As she stood alone she said: "Oh, the weight that rolled on my mind for my dear children, and how I should bring them up in the nurture and admonition of the Lord." Her great desire was that the affliction might be sanctified to her and to them. But she tells us that for ten weeks she prayed in great sorrow and with mourning and weeping before God. Her own words are: "The grief of my heart no tongue can tell. The dearest comfort of my life taken from me, I felt myself stripped of all earthly comforts, and my Lord hid his face from me." She felt that she could bear all things if she might but once more feel the fullness of her Saviour's presence. And she tells us that after weeks of sorrow, at the communion-table, he was made known to her in the breaking of bread. She heard him say: "Return, O backsliding daughter, for I am married to thee!"

Now she had new and precious views of the union of believers with Christ their head. In relating the experience of those days, at one point she says: "The Spirit of God worked powerfully upon me. I wanted nothing but to see the glory of God and see and feel his Spirit poured out more and more on myself and others." At one time after wrestling for hours for souls, she tells us that she "went to rest and slept very quietly till some time in the night, when," she says, "I waked with these words running through my mind with great sweetness, Wonderful — Counselor — the mighty God — the everlasting Father — the Prince of

Peace. I can not describe the joy and peace that succeeded."

Miss Lyon valued her mother's prayers above all earthly treasures, and she learned their worth while yet a little child, when that mother often tarried long in the closet, and, coming forth, would sink down upon her bed exhausted, while the older sister would whisper to the little ones, "I think there is going to be an awakening."

Eternity alone can reveal the connection between the prayers of this mother in Israel, and the many precious revivals of religion, in which the daughter was permitted to labor. Never can we forget the deep emotion of that daughter, as she said, in 1840, "I have no longer a mother to pray for me and my dear pupils." She rests from her prayers, but they do follow her.

CHAPTER II.

Home Duties and Training.

GOD'S WAYS OF PREPARING HIS PEOPLE FOR SERVICE — "THE BACK SIDE OF THE DESERT" — THE THREE CORNERS — THE WIDOW AND HER HOME — THE HOMESPUN DRESS — SPINNING AND WEAVING — HOUSEHOLD DUTIES — THE WIDOW'S GARDEN — INFLUENCE OF CHRISTIAN HOMES — HER MOTHER'S RE-MARRIAGE — HER ELDEST BROTHER — MARY HIS HOUSEKEEPER — HER CONVERSION AND CONSECRATION TO CHRIST.

IN a letter written by one of Miss Lyon's pupils long years since, we find the following: "I have just been looking out the passages which were read to us this morning from Miss Lyon's Bible; and when she reads to us, it always seems to me that there are treasures in her Bible that were left out of mine. But as usual I have found all, and here they are: "Now Moses kept the flock of Jethro his father-in-law. And Moses was content to dwell with the man. And he led the flock to the back side of the desert. And when forty years were expired, there appeared unto him in the wilderness of Sinai an angel of the Lord, in a flame of fire in a bush. The same Moses did

God send to be a ruler and deliverer." Her subject was, "God's ways of preparing individuals for service in his church."

She said: "When God has a great work for any one to do in the world, he usually gives him a peculiar training for it; and that training is just what no earthly friend would choose for him, and sometimes it is so long continued that there seems to us to be but little time left for him to work. *We* should not have led Moses into Midian to prepare him to guide a nation, and certainly we should not have left him there forty years. But God knew that the life of the humble shepherd, and in the desert too, would best fit him to lead his people like a flock, and that he needed to be in that school no less than forty long years to be the truly meek Moses. He who was to bring water out of the rock for all Israel, must first humble himself to draw, and perhaps many times, water for the sheep of the daughters of Jethro. He who was to receive offerings for the tabernacle till he should say, 'Let neither man nor woman make any more offering,' must needs know what some of these cost, by seeing the daughters of Midian spin and dye with their own hands. He must have long years of quiet, under the shadow of Sinai, for meditation on the character of God, before he could meet that God on the top of the mount, and there receive the lively oracles to give unto us.

"I can not tell you, young ladies, how I felt while pondering this Scripture this morning. It did seem to me most delightful to feel that we may be led of God all the time, and, like Moses, we should be content with the place where he bids us dwell. I doubt not that some of you may feel that you have been, and even now are, kept back from the greatest usefulness. The sickness of friends, and other circumstances, may have hindered you in your studies, and may be you sometimes long for wealth, and other friends to help you rise in life. I would not have you feel thus, but rather use very carefully all that the Lord gives you. And don't be afraid of the 'back side of the desert,' and never think you are forsaken of God because kept long there. He knows just how much of quiet, humble life we need to serve him in the best manner hereafter. The man who cared faithfully for the sheep in the desert, led Israel to Canaan; and he who kept 'those few sheep in the wilderness' was afterwards Israel's king and sweetest singer."

We can hardly feel less interest in Mary Lyon's early home, where Conway, Ashfield, and Buckland made the "Three Corners," than in Moses dwelling in the desert. Her twenty years in that "mountain home" were as surely the Lord's preparation for guiding the thousands of the daughters of America, as were Moses' forty years in the wilderness a preparation for leading the thousands of Israel. In that pure mountain air, among those hills and streams and the rocks and the trees, she acquired that physical strength which enabled her to bear a pressure of labor and care in after life that might have carried others to an early grave. And there, in the care of a mother, who, she tells us, "was a sort of presiding angel of good works in all that little neighborhood, and whose cheerful spirit helped not a little to make her brow as noble and as lofty at forty as on her bridal day," she learned to love all, and to have so much of cheerfulness and sunshine in her heart, that Dr. Hitchcock could say, after thirty years' acquaintance: "Never did I see a cloud on her countenance."

That "wild, romantic, little farm, made more to feast the soul than to feed the body," on which was that little mountain home, yielded so abundantly, under the widowed mother's care, that none of her seven children "ever thought of being dependent or depressed," least of all the sunny-faced Mary.

The simple school-day dress, so neat and clean, satisfied her, and she learned its worth as she watched the growing flax, and later saw the hired man or her own brother break and swingle, and, may be, hatchel it, and then saw it wound upon the distaff of the little wheel, and her own mother spinning the web. She longed to help her, but they told her that "little girls must learn to spin filling before warp;" and so the mother made the warp, and Mary the filling, at "the great wheel," from the rolls that had been carded for her. Then came the day for dyeing the linen. The little country store furnished the indigo or copperas, as might be called for, and the farm contributed other excellent dye-stuffs, in the form of birch-bark, peach-leaves, and smart-weed. Then she saw it spooled and warped and woven in the loom in her own home, where she could watch that same mother as she "sprung the treadle," and "threw the shuttle," and Mary wound all the quills till the work was done. We do not wonder that she was satisfied with such a dress for those bright summer days; and then the winter dress was of hardly less interest to her, for she watched the sheep-shearing, the wool-picking and washing, the sending of the wool to the carding-machine, and the sacks of rolls as they were returned. Again there was spinning, in which Mary had a large share. Sometimes that "unbanding wheel" would trouble her; then the mother would sing to her,

> "It's not in the wheel, it's not in the band, —
> It's in the girl who takes it in hand."

And so the girl who took it in hand learned many a valuable lesson for life at the wheel. Weaving again followed spinning; the cloth was sent to the mill, and the bright red flannel came home for the winter dress, in which she was never afraid of the snow. The pretty linen aprons of blue and white check, from the same piece with the mother' short-gown, more than satisfied her. And who could wish better shoes than the tanner and currier and neighborhood shoemaker produced from the skin of their own fatted calf?

She helped her mother make the butter, which they sold at the store for sixpence a pound, to buy the "rare gift of the Sunday suit, kept expressly for the occasion," and which, she says, "formed an era in the life of the possessor, and was remembered with grateful smiles for many days to come." She helped make the blankets, and bedquilts too, and last, but not least, the summer and winter coverlet, from which, she used to tell us, she learned many a valuable lesson in the building and arranging of Mt. Holyoke Seminary.

We did not understand all she said about it, but we remember just what she said: "For you know, young ladies, it had a blue side for winter, and a white side for summer, so we could use it all the year round."

She was learning valuable lessons also, as she stood by her mother's side, sorting and arranging those little autumnal stores that were to travel hand in hand through the long winter, like the barrel of meal and cruse of oil in another widow's home; and when there came a season in which the sugar-orchard gave only fifty pounds of maple-sugar instead of the two hundred it was accustomed to give, she saw that even that would not fail before the warm sun and the sparkling snow told that sugar-days were again near. Often there was a pound of sugar, a basket of apples, or some other good thing to be sent to one who had failed to gather manna enough for the winter, and that one would ask: "How is it the widow can do more for me than any one else?" We find the answer to this inquiry in her own words, which thousands have heard fall from those lips that ever opened in wisdom: "Comfort and economy, good taste, and true Christian liberality, may be found together, but their union requires rare forethought and good judgment." "Never destroy any thing that God has made, or given skill to others to make." "Never think any thing worthless till it has done all the good it can." "Economy and self-denial are the two great springs which feed the fountains of benevolence. Practice them for Christ's sake, but talk very little about them." "Be very thankful for a little, and you will receive the more."

The sweet little garden, loved as soon as seen, was proverbial in that section, and more than one asked to place rare plants in it, "because nothing ever died in widow Lyon's garden." There was a lesson learned there, which led her in after years to care for every plant in her garden; and not a few felt that what they placed there *must* live for ever. She tells us that "the roses, the pinks, and peonies, which keep time with Old Hundred, could nowhere grow so fresh and so sweet as in that little garden." "And nowhere else, did she ever see wild strawberries in such profusion and richness as were gathered in those little baskets." "Nowhere else were rare-ripes so large and so yellow, and never were peaches so delicious and so fair as grew on the trees of that little farm; and the apples too contrived to ripen before all others, so as to meet in sweet fellowship with peaches and plums, to entertain the aunts and the cousins." Where, better than there, could she have learned that comfort may be found closely joined with economy and liberality?

There was not a nook or corner of that little farm or house which was not loved by Mary, and from which she did not draw lessons for the future. A few years before she was called to her heavenly home, she wrote: "How sweet did I find it once more to linger around the dearest scenes of that loved spot, long since laid up among the cherished jewels of memory's most sacred casket!" She thanked God that her father was spared to her for six years. It was a brief period, to be sure, but none of us, who have ever heard her talk of a father's love can doubt her feeling its sacred influence; and we believed that her little heart had trusted and obeyed a father too, when we heard her say: "Young ladies, be very slow to depart from a Christian father's counsel. In your father you have a divinely appointed safeguard; trust him, lean upon him, and there learn your relation to your heavenly Father. If you can lose your will in your father's, you will much more easily say, 'Not my will, but thine be done, my Father in heaven.'"

She often said to her pupils: "There is nothing more pleasant on earth than a cultivated, refined, well-organized Christian family." She knew well the blessed influence of such a family, for she says of her home: "Nothing there was left to take its own way. Every thing was made to yield to the mother's faithful, diligent hand. Early and late she was engaged in the culture of the olive-plants around her table." As she watched her, she found, to use her own words, that "a mother, whose time and thoughts are necessarily engrossed with the care of her family, may yet have much enjoyment in God."

When the Christian father had gone to his rest, there was still a family altar in that house, though Mary calls it a "bereaved family altar," but adds: "What child of that household can ever forget the extraordinary prayers of that sorrowing mother for the salvation of her fatherless children, as they were offered up day by day through that first, long, cold winter of widowhood?" As one after another of those dear children were brought to Christ, till they could not only say We are seven, but We are seven in the fold, that mother's agonizing prayers were remembered even by Mary, then the little one of six years. We seem to see that mother, in what we once heard Miss Lyon say in her school: "Our grandmothers were not house-keepers *only*. True, they read but few books, but they read those thoroughly, thought deeply, and many of them had much mental culture." Miss Lyon always desired to make her schools strictly family schools, for she said: "Young ladies can nowhere be so well cared for as in the family. There the government may be so mild, yet so undeviating and inflexible, that there will only be advice on the part of the parents, and compliance on the part of the child." This gives another picture of that home, and we have yet another when she looks back and says: "I can see through a veil of forty years, in that mountain home, growing on the perennial stalk of great principles, the buddings of sentiments, of customs, and of habits, which, if spread over the country and fanned by the gentle breezes of intelligence, influence, and Christian sympathy, would produce a rich and abundant harvest to the treasury of the Lord." And we may add, they *have* produced not only a rich harvest for the treasury of the Lord, but abundant fruit for the garner of eternal life.

Mary loved and honored her mother; and she only asks her pupils to be like herself, when she says: "Let your letters to your mother be a picture of a warm-hearted, loving, confiding daughter. Bestow your choicest expressions of affection upon your mother." With such feelings, we do not wonder that her young heart was tried to have that mother leave the mountain home, in 1810, when Mary was only thirteen years of age, take her two little sisters with her, assume another name, and find her abode in Ashfield. We never heard her speak of this but once, and then she said: "I would not let it make me unhappy. I found I could love my new father; he was very kind to me. My mother was relieved of much care. I really became very happy." The experience of her early life led her to feel most tenderly for the widow and fatherless, and she often said: "I do not wonder God speaks so frequently of them." Oh! how her face used to glow with more of heaven than earth when she added: "My father and mother forsook me, but the Lord took me up."

After her mother's marriage, she learned, as never before, the worth of her only and older brother. For nine years her home was with him at the old homestead. She could say most truly, "For me he careth;" and she no less carefully sought to make his interests her own. Before his marriage, and when only fifteen years of age, she was his house-keeper. She performed all the work of that farm-house, and he gave her a dollar a week for it. If we remember rightly, he paid her all in silver dollars. But be this as it may, we know she used to say: "I never saw any such dollars before, nor have I since. They were mine, and my dear brother had given them to me. I did weep over them." After his marriage, she was still a member of his family, and no one was more welcome there than Mary. In those nine years with that brother she learned much of Jesus, the elder Brother. As we have heard her talk of him with streaming eyes, and been led by her to look to a Brother in heaven on our Father's right hand, we have said: "It is a blessed thing to be led of God to the back side of the desert, for that is surely close by the mount of holy vision."

She often said to us: "We must follow the family plan if we would have a good school. In the family we get the first ideas of right and wrong, and there the most correct ideas of mutual relations, of obedience to authority, of treating equals with respect and affection." And then she would add: "We thank God that the last thing sin can do is to break up the family circle. It is wonderful how much better we are made by these family relations. The little child makes the father a better man, and the excellences of a woman are nowhere so marked, and they nowhere shine so beautifully, as in the wife and mother." Then, with a seeming glimpse of the great family in heaven, she would say: "If there is so much that is delightful where there is sin, what must that state be, where there is no more sin! What hallowed, what sublime affections shall we behold there!"

In her brother's family she found great comfort in caring for his children, and it was a sore trial to her to give them up in 1819, when they removed to Western New York. We are thankful that she could have them so long with her, and, as she used to say of others, "become more Christ-like by loving little children." The infant of a few days, or even hours, was very precious in her sight. We seem even now to see her bending over her sister's sick and dying bed, whose babe had preceded her to the eternal world, and saying: "Be thankful, dear, that you have given another little one for the ransomed throng."

It was a beautiful Sabbath afternoon of May, 1816, in which Mary Lyon first said, with full heart, "Abba, Father," "Jesus *my* Saviour." Her home was there in the humble cottage at the foot of the hill. She had that day, as was her wont, mingled with the worshippers in the little Baptist church of the Three Corners. Good old Elder Smith talked, both morning and afternoon, of the character and government of God. At the close of the last service, the silver-haired man rose to bless his flock. He gazed upon them for a moment with more than paternal interest, and then said, with deep solemnity: "Remember, my friends, it is a fearful thing, and a very wicked thing too, not to love such a God as I have told you about to-day." The fatherly hand was raised, — there was heard, "Grace, mercy, and peace be with you *all*," — and the congregation scattered. Mary took the "wild, winding way" to her home. She trod that way but slowly, for her heart was too full for a hurried footstep. As she approached the dwelling, an inexpressible feeling of tenderness stole over her. She remembered a scene in the "north room," thirteen years before, when, a little child of six years, she heard her dying father say with faltering voice: "My dear children, — what shall I say to you, my children? God bless you, my children!" — and then he was parted from them to enter into the fullness of blessing. The never-to-be-forgotten prayers of her mother passed before her, and she exclaimed: "Why should I not be blessed of my parents' God?" — and turned away from her home to the hill-side, to be alone with the eternal One. She dwelt upon his wisdom, holiness, mercy, and justice, till peace came to her troubled soul, and she exclaimed: "O God! thy ways *are* perfect; be thou *my*

Father, and the guide of my youth, my everlasting portion."

Her heart now melted in love to him who had brought her to his Father and her Father, and, led by that elder Brother, she went to the hill-top near by. She looked thence upon the far-off mountains in all their grandeur, on the deep valleys with the widely extended plains, and the smiling villages below, and then thought of the kingdoms of the world, and, to use her own words, "longed to lay them all at the feet of Him who had redeemed her." Twelve years afterward she wrote: "I remember that moment as though it were but yesterday." As well she might; for then, and there, she was not only born anew, but baptized into a love for souls which made her so much like her divine Master that she was continually straitened till her thirty-three years of labor for souls were accomplished, and she beheld her Father, God, and Saviour in unvailed glory.

CHAPTER III.

Early School Days.

MARY'S FIRST SCHOOL — "BOARDING ROUND" — HER POPULARITY — HER WAGES — THE SECRET OF GOVERNMENT — IS A PUPIL IN SANDERSON'S ACADEMY — SUPPORTS HERSELF BY LABOR — LEARNS THE LATIN GRAMMAR IN THREE DAYS — "WINGS POTATOES" — RECEIVES TUITION FREE — IN AMHERST ACADEMY — STUDY OF THE SCIENCES — HER UNSELFISHNESS — MEMORIES OF THOSE SCHOOL-DAYS PRESERVED — CHILDREN OF HER SCHOOLMATES SENT TO BE HER PUPILS.

MARY commenced her work as a teacher when about seventeen years of age, at Shelburne Falls, Mass. She was paid seventy-five cents per week for her services, and received in addition her board. But it was understood that she was to "board round." And she used in after years to tell her pupils how happy she was in dividing up her school term, and finding that she must board "just five days for each scholar;" and how, when one family was not quite ready to have the school-ma'am come to board, nother was, and so her bread was always sure.

We have loved to listen to those parents as they have told us how "she helped the children so much out of school that they would not have cared much, if they had boarded her all the time for nothing." She was in families where they sought wool and flax, and wrought willingly; where hands were laid to the spindle and held the distaff; and where they made their own fine linen. The new teacher rose rapidly in the estimation of her employers, when it was whispered in the neighborhood that she had been teaching one of the daughters how to bring out damask from the old hand-loom. She could tell her how to "draw in" the web into the old twine "harness," never failing to put "front wing," "back wing," and "middle wing," in their right place. That daughter soon after found a home in a distant part of our country, but she always loved to speak of Mary Lyon, and to tell her children how, when in trouble with her tangled web, she said to her: "Perhaps I can help you, — I'll try." The lady was not surprised to hear in after years of her success in teaching, — of her winning hearts to herself and to Christ; for she said: "Even then she was so full of benevolence we were all drawn to her," and she might have added Miss Lyon's own remark: "The same amount of talent will rise higher with benevolence."

But the teacher was not as well satisfied with her success as were her employers, and she has told us that she resolved many times, during that long summer, if once safely through, never to teach again. She devised her way, but the Lord directed her steps. She continued this occupation, and years afterward was accustomed to say to her pupils: "If you commence teaching, and do not succeed, teach till you *do* succeed." She ever thanked the Lord that she began her experience in this capacity, "boarding round," and feeling that she was worth only three dollars a month.

With such a beginning, always giving herself unreservedly to her pupils, and, after going to South Hadley, never receiving more than two hundred dollars per year, she could well say: "Ladies should not expect a large compensation for teaching. They should go into the work with the same motives with which the servant of the Lord goes into the ministry." Sometimes she would so talk to her pupils of the blessedness of teaching, the reward in heaven, and the reward even on earth, in the love of grateful hearts, that it would seem to them a most delightful privilege to give their lives to teaching. Perhaps at this point she would add: "I hardly expect many of you to give your lives to teaching; but she who can teach well, control the minds of the young happily and rightly, is all the better prepared for every sphere to which a lady can be called. But if you teach, never expect to govern others till you can govern yourself."

Her one power in controlling pupils was found here. She had learned, in that mountain home, to yield her own will to others, and feeling that she had not attained, or was already perfect, she went on practicing her own maxim: "Self-control is never perfect, till we can cheerfully meet our own government. Nor is a child really governed till he can smile under government." She had herself smiled under her mother's authority, and afterward been delighted with God's government, exclaiming, "It is perfect!" and now her first little pupils smiled under hers; while many have been made happy for life and for eternity, because they learned with her, "It is easier to obey God than any one else."

We are not aware that Miss Lyon had herself attended any other than just such a district school as the one she taught herself, till the autumn of 1817. Then she entered Sanderson's Academy, Ashfield. Her scanty means would not allow of her paying for both board and tuition here; so she sought to defray the expense of the former by the labor of her own hands.

Here she so distinguished herself as a scholar that it was not teachers and pupils alone that honored and spoke to one another of her. "That Mary Lyon" was talked of all over Ashfield Plains. It was even then matter of speculation what manner of woman she would be who could learn the Latin grammar in *three* days, and be able to recite in almost every class in school.

It is said that a good man in the place one morning met the gentleman with whom she boarded, when he said: "Well, this Mary Lyon is a wonderful girl,— isn't she? They say that none of the boys can keep up with her. But how is it about her work? Does she really do any thing, or do you just about give her her board?"

"Well," said her friend, "Mary wings the potatoes!"

We do not exactly know whether he intended to praise her, but he opens to us the good, old-fashioned farm-house where she boarded; the great open fireplace with its generous back-log, and fine bed of hot ashes in front, where the potatoes were often and well roasted. We can see her, wing in hand, bending over the smoking pile of potatoes, just unburied, and winging each so well that no one who sat at that table wished there was a better way to cook their potatoes.

Many will ever thank the good people of Ashfield who gave her potatoes to wing; and more will thank the noble trustees of Sanderson Academy, who subsequently gave her free tuition, when she was about to return to spinning and weaving, to help her go forward in her studies. She felt herself in no small degree indebted to them and other Ashfield friends, from whom she says: "I received many acts of unfeigned friendship while creeping my way along toward a humble place in my Master's service."

Mary Lyon always remembered with interest a term in Amherst Academy, where her love for the study of the sciences was gratified beyond what it had been in any previous school. She gathered knowledge there, as her room-mate said she afterward did in Byfield, "by handfulls." She delighted herself particularly in chemistry while in Amherst, as she did later with Professor Eaton in Troy; and those who were privileged to study it with her in after years knew she had learned it well. They can never forget those successful experiments, those clear explanations; and they love still to refer to their seventy pages of notes on "Miss Lyon's chemical lectures," found in the marble-covered books of her time. And there are other marble-covered books which show how she turned from lecture-room to hall, there to dwell more impressively than ever on the character of the wonderful God, and the blessedness of dwelling for ever with him, studying those ways which are now past finding out.

Mary Lyon found time, and had a heart, for kindness as well as study, when in Amherst. She always delighted there, as she had done elsewhere, to aid those less successful in study than herself. She chose some retired place for doing it, and it was always in a way that made the person aided feel that she would be glad to have her know all she knew. A daughter of one who was a member of Amherst Academy with Miss

Lyon says: "When a little girl, my mother used to sit and tell us about Mary Lyon at school. She would make us see just how she looked in her linsey-woolsey dress, and how ready she was to give a kind look and a loving heart to every one. She was always to be found, out of school hours, in her favorite corner, studying as hard as she could, but ready to help every one that cared to be helped. If any one wished to change her seat in the school-room, 'Oh! I will change with you, — I would like to do it, if you prefer my seat,' would be heard from Mary Lyon's lips. If there was an undesirable seat-mate in all the school, she was always ready to sit by her, and help her on her way, even though it was on a window-seat; and mother would add: 'Do you wonder, my little girls, that we all loved and respected Mary Lyon?'"

When that mother came to die, one of her last requests was: "Send my daughters to Mary Lyon's school." Many a father has heard the same request from his departing companion. We know of one, an Israelite indeed, who has successively placed six daughters under her instruction because their mother, with heaven in full view, said: "Promise me that these dear girls shall be placed in Miss Lyon's school." The father promised and fulfilled; and the last of the six daughters there learned to love the Saviour a few weeks before Miss Lyon went to be with the sainted mother. It often seemed as if there was not a school on earth where were so many daughters of mothers passed into heaven. And when we saw the truly maternal love there given them, we did not wonder that the dying mother, with her eye upon Jesus and her hand already in his, should have been directed by him to whisper Mary Lyon's name as the guardian of her children on earth.

More than once, when some one of Miss L.'s young teachers would beg that some wayward girl might be removed from school, have we heard the reply with tears in her eyes: "Do you know —— 's mother was a very dear friend of mine. I seem to hear her ask me from heaven if I can not do a little more for her child. Do you not think, Miss ——, you can bear with her a little longer?" And then her countenance would light up, and she would add: "She is a child of prayer. Don't forget that." One loved to labor, encouraged by such words; and many of those daughters have been blessed in "Mary Lyon's school." But the seeds of this blessing were sown when Miss Lyon was the self-sacrificing, self-forgetting pupil in Buckland, Ashfield, Amherst, and Byfield; and it was doubtless in remembrance of those days that she used to say to us in after years: "Young ladies, never ask to live simply for yourselves. Live for the good of others, and you will find your cup of happiness run ning over, even in this world; and oh, what will it be in heaven! Be willing to do any thing and go any where for the good of others, and remember that you are responsible for elevating the character of every one with whom you have to do."

CHAPTER IV.

At Byfield and Derry.

ADVICE ON THE LATE COMPLETION OF AN EDUCATION— OPPOSITION TC MISS LYON'S GOING TO BYFIELD — HER DESCRIPTION OF THE JOURNEY THITHER — HOME-SICKNESS — MR. EMERSON'S INSTRUCTIONS — HIS RESPECT FOR WOMAN'S TALENTS — HIS VIEW OF HER PROPER STATION — THE TRUE OBJECT OF AN EDUCATION, "TO DO GOOD" — RETURN TO ASHFIELD — TEACHING IN SANDERSON'S ACADEMY — PROFESSION OF RELIGION — ENGAGEMENT WITH MISS GRANT IN DERRY, N. H. — PRINCIPLES INTRODUCED INTO THE SCHOOL — STUDY OF THE SCRIPTURES — ATTACHMENT TO MISS G.

IN 1821, when Mary was twenty-four years of age, she found her way to Byfield, Mass., to enjoy the instructions of Rev. Joseph Emerson, principal of Byfield Academy. It should here be said that Miss Lyon did not advise young ladies under her care ordinarily to defer completing their education to so late a period. She used to say to us: "I don't want you to spin and weave because I did. It was best for me to do it; but you may be thankful that this necessity is removed, and that you may be able to finish your studies earlier, and thus have more time to work for the Lord. I thank God every day for the hope and the expectation, too, that you will do a great deal more than I have done in the world;" and the dear woman's face would shine when she said this, something as we imagine Moses' to have shone when he came down from the mount; but, like him, she knew it not.

But we were speaking of Mr. E.'s school at Byfield. Like other good things, it cost Miss Lyon a great deal to go there, not only of money, but of the richest treasures of the heart. When she first proposed "to go to Byfield to school," she hardly found a friend to encourage her in the desire. Most of the good people around her thought she already knew a great deal. They were sure she "had learning enough to teach their daughters;" and, as she "never would be a minister, why should she go off to Byfield to school?" But her mother said, "Go, my child." We suspect she had already done what she afterward said all daughters should do, "come up fully to their mothers' standard, and thus invite those mothers to higher and higher endeavors and nobler aspirations." With her parents' approbation she left home; and we must permit her to tell her own story of the journey as she once gave it to us in the school-room.

"You can hardly understand, young ladies, what a great thing it was to get to Byfield. It was almost like going to Europe now. Why, it took us *three* long days to go from Ashfield to Byfield. Good Esq. White, who was one of my fathers, took me in his own carriage with his daughter.* I was really a little homesick the second night, when I realized that I was so far from home. You will laugh, and you *may* laugh, for I am going to tell you that the next day I was really *very* homesick. We lost our way, and I did not know as we ever should find the noted Byfield, for the good people near Boston did not seem to know very well where it was. And can you believe it, young ladies, Miss W. and I both cried! I cried just as hard as I could; and I really think I outcried my friend, whose good father smiled upon us. But we found Byfield,—for Esq. White did something better than weep; and when he went back to Ashfield, he told our friends that he had left us in a good place, and that we would come home the next fall." Greatly interested in her story of finding Byfield, we were always glad afterward to hear her refer to the school and its teacher.

Miss Lyon has herself told us of the buddings of sentiments, of customs and habits in her "mountain home," waiting only the fanning of "the gentle breezes of intelligence, influence, and Christian sympathy," to bring forth the choicest fruits. These were truly fanned by "good Mr. Emerson," and they were yielding daily fruit years afterward, when she used to say:

* Amanda White, afterward wife of Rev. Mr. Ferry, missionary to Mackinaw.

"My dear teacher, *now* in heaven, said and thought thus."

Miss Lyon, in her first acquaintance with him, was impressed with Mr. Emerson's high regard for woman's intellectual powers, and this impression was strengthened, as she observed from day to day his manner of treating his pupils and other ladies. She says: "If a lady advanced an opinion to which he could not assent, he did not hesitate to object because it was the opinion of a *lady;* for he appeared to believe that she had a mind capable of weighing an argument, and that she would gratefully receive the correction of an error. The tendency of the course he pursued was to inspire ladies with a modest confidence, not only in their own individual powers, but also in the native abilities of their sex, and to give them those just views of their real worth, which are so suited to lead them to dislike and avoid all mean pretensions to knowledge, genius, and greatness; and to do away the assumption that they were never designed to be literary or scientific, and that they can not be, without injury to themselves and others." With Mr. E., she regarded the jewel of learning "in a woman without discretion," just as Solomon regards that of beauty, and was equally desirous to repress a disgusting vanity and to inspire a proper confidence. She said: "In a mixed company, I never knew him, having talked in a profitable and interesting manner and on some practical subject with a circle of gentlemen, on one hand, to turn his attention to a circle of ladies, on the other, and descend to needless commonplace inquiries and trifling remarks. In conversation with him, ladies generally had a feeling of being regarded like equals as well as friends. There was no needless gallantry, no apparent consciousness of stooping, or of condescension. His sincere and unfeigned regard for the sex was told far less by words than by his cordial, familiar, and unaffected manner." With such an example as Mr. Emerson, and with his views made her own, it is not strange that Miss Lyon sought earnestly to raise woman to the place she believed God designed her to occupy, and as fully believed man would give her if she should prove herself worthy of it. She believed, with Mr. E., "that in some things which are not necessary to enable" woman "to fulfill her varied and extensive duties, her strength of intellect is not equal to that of the other sex; but that in other things no less noble, and equally important for the good of the world, she excels." She learned to think, with him, that the station of woman "is designed by Providence to be subordinate and dependent, to a degree far exceeding the difference in native talents." She could rejoice in this, because she regarded it "as dictated by infinite wisdom and goodness, not for the elevation of the one, or for the depression of the other, but for the promotion of the greatest good of the whole." Miss Lyon gave such sentiments to her pupils long after Mr. Emerson had gone to his heavenly home, adding: "He gave them to me, and I am sure he drew them from the Bible: they are the Bible itself." Sometimes, going a step further, she would add: "While he thought that the wife owes to her husband obedience, modified and limited by the laws of God, he did not consider it the duty of the husband in any ordinary case to command. If in families, so wonderfully fitted in their very organization to be the abode of happiness and love, there may be found here and there an instance of strange alienation and discord, how many more such scenes should we witness, if the Bible had clothed each part of the united head with equal authority to rule! The obedience which Mr. Emerson would inculcate would be so genuine and unaffected as scarcely to be recognized as such by either party, the whole being clothed in the beautiful robe of mutual respect and esteem." Miss Lyon had seen just what is here described in her own home, and was all ready to be benefited by such words, and to make them bring forth abundant fruit in her many pupils. In her description of Mr. Emerson's character, she says: "Any lady — and the cases are not rare — who has occasion to excel in guiding her household; in being the active head of all her various departments of domestic labor; in presiding in the parlor and at the table without display or diffidence; in rendering her house the abode of hospitality as well as of domestic happiness; in becoming a skillful teacher for her own children and for others who may be gathered into the Sabbath school or Bible class; and in being the mainspring of many a benevolent association; and, beside all, who finds it desirable to be intelligent on most subjects of practical interest, and it may be, too, to be literary without vanity, and scientific without ostentation, — any lady, who has occasion for all this, will have great reason for gratitude that she ever enjoyed the privilege of sitting under the instruction of my dearly beloved and highly revered teacher."

Miss Lyon was often heard to thank God for directing her to the place where she learned the true object of education, — to do good. She brought with her from Byfield, Mr. Emerson's views of the study of Scripture, and both she and Miss Grant carried them out more fully than their teacher was able to do himself. The same was true of prayer-meetings, laboring for souls, and seeking to save a world.

Miss Lyon returned from Byfield in the autumn, and engaged again as teacher in Sanderson's Academy in Ashfield, "grateful," as she said, "to do a little for the school that had done so much for her." In the spring of 1822, she united with the Congregational church in Buckland, upon profession of her faith. She continued in the same employment two years longer, when Providence opened the way for her to be associated with Miss Grant in the Adams Female Academy in Londonderry (now Derry), New Hampshire. She had become interested in that school through others, and had sometimes asked, when alone with the Lord, if it might not be possible that Miss Grant should do a work for him in L. She had never expressed this, which she called "a romantic thought;" but her heavenly Father heeded the unuttered desire. In later years, when she better knew her dear Father's love, she regarded it as an evidence of her having enjoyed "sweet fellowship of thought with him." When, a few days afterward, she received a letter from Miss Grant, she broke the seal, glanced at the contents, and, finding that the latter had really been invited to take charge of the school, she exclaimed: "Is this a dream, or is it a reality?" A little later there came a request from her dear friend that she would join with her in labor. She looked up and said: "Speak, Lord, for thy servant heareth." To Miss Grant she wrote: "The prospect since you first wrote me has appeared sufficiently pleasant; indeed, I fear too pleasant. I tremble more than if the path appeared more rugged." Miss Lyon had learned, when in Byfield, to esteem and love Miss Grant most highly, and, loving her thus, she was rejoiced to help her carry forward that school. Mr. Emerson's principles, modified to meet the wants of the pupils, were here acted upon. Miss Lyon was delighted to find that her friend had made such an arrangement with her employers as to feel at liberty to use one seventh part of the intellectual energies of her pupils upon what is contained in that storehouse of knowledge, the Scriptures. The Bible was studied every day in that school. There were recitations every Monday, and, some parts of the term, every day; and, after months of trial, Miss Lyon says this study had excited deeper and more universal interest than any other; and just so she found it in all her schools in after years. "It gave pupils," to use her own words, "intellectual discipline, guidance, and control over the heart, and they really loved their Bible lessons."

Miss Lyon ever spoke of those months in Derry as an important part of her preparation for long years of teaching. She valued Miss Grant's counsels and experience, and she prized a friend to whom she could give her warmest affections. We well remember the lesson of love we learned from Miss Lyon a score of years afterward, when she was telling us of her happy connection with Miss Grant. She spoke from a feeling heart when she said: "Some suppose the strength of affection is greater in youth than in advanced life. This may be true of worldly love, but not of Christian love. Young ladies, I want you to love so tenderly, so deeply, that the roots will not be found spread upon the surface alone. Let them strike into your inmost souls. You need not fear loving too ardently, if you only love in Christ. You may show too much fondness for your friends in public, but you are in no danger of giving them too much true affection. Do you not think I can and do love Miss Grant better than when we taught together in Derry?" We all believed her. One of her teachers wrote, during an examination at Mount Holyoke: "I think I never saw Miss Lyon look so happy as she did to-day, when Miss Curtis whispered to her on the platform, 'Mrs. Banister (Miss Grant) has come.' She excused herself for a few moments, and soon returned with Mrs. Banister and placed her by her side, to tell us all, by her very manner, that a near and very dear friend had arrived.' This was the love of advanced life.

CHAPTER V.

The Buckland School.

RETURN FROM DERRY IN THE AUTUMN OF 1824 — TEACHES IN BUCKLAND THE NEXT WINTER — INFLUENCE OF HER SCHOOL — DESIRE FOR ITS CONTINUANCE THE WINTER FOLLOWING — THE TUITION FEE — PAYING IN ADVANCE — OPENING OF THE SCHOOL — HOMESICKNESS — COLBURN'S ARITHMETIC — BIBLE STUDIES — BEGINNING OF RELIGIOUS INTEREST AMONG THE PUPILS — THE REVIVAL — ITS FRUITS.

MISS LYON had passed thirty weeks of 1824 most happily and profitably with Miss G. at Derry, when the school was closed for the winter.

She returned to Buckland, where she had, the next winter, a little school of twenty-five young ladies. Most of the pupils boarded with their parents, and Miss Lyon found a home in the family of the pastor, Rev. Mr. Clarke. This school was little known in the vicinity that winter, but its influence worked quietly all summer, and many Christian parents, who were waiting for salvation to come to Israel, were heard to ask before another winter: "Is it certain that Miss Lyon will come back from Derry" (whither she had again gone), "and teach here next year? We do hope she will; for our daughters need just such a school. Why did we not know of hers last winter?" They prayed and waited, and soon they heard, "She will almost certainly come." And before November had gone by, it was said, "She has come." Yes, she was there in season to make all her arrangements.

The young ladies were to assemble on Tuesday after Thanksgiving. There was no newspaper notice of the day, and none was needed; for the last year's pupils had not only well advertised the school and teacher, but made everybody understand that school would commence Wednesday, precisely at nine o'clock; and all those who would enjoy most of Miss Lyon's approving smile had better be there Tuesday night. The girls of the surrounding towns had hoped for a Thanksgiving-day snow to take them to Buckland, but it did not come; and so, early Tuesday morning, the great wagons were brought out, and fathers and mothers were busy in planning to keep their daughters warm on their way over the frozen ground. They did not like, after what they had heard, to wait till Wednesday, though it was about certain it would snow before night, and be good sleighing the next morning.

Miss Lyon was all ready for them. She had concluded to make her charge for tuition only a shilling a week; and the good people in Buckland, in full sympathy with her spirit, thought they could board for five shillings a week; and so she said to the fathers, as they brought in their daughters: "We plan to have our term fourteen weeks; and, as Mr. G. wants to help on this work, he will board so cheaply that board and tuition for the term will be only fourteen dollars. Perhaps you had better give them a few dollars for their books, etc., but they will not need a great deal." One father, on hearing this, drew out his old black pocket-book, — the very embodiment of "Owe no man any thing," — and said: "You will allow me to pay you in advance." "Well, sir, I think you had better not," she replied. "Perhaps your daughter will not like us well enough to stay;" and then, turning to the bright-eyed daughter, she added: "though I think she will; but we shall not need the money at once. You will come over and see us after a few weeks, and you can give it to us then if we find we do want it." That father saw Miss Lyon for one moment alone, to tell her that possibly his daughter might wish to direct her own studies; but Miss Lyon did not allow him to finish his story; for, beginning to pass hand over hand most rapidly, she said, "Oh, sir, I don't think we shall have any trouble. I presume we shall get along very nicely." Her manner, in not allowing him to tell her that his daughter had even a single fault, was understood by that discerning parent. He trusted her with his whole heart. He had no more to say; and, giving his good-by to teacher and daughter, he turned away to give place to other equally anxious fathers, all of whom were satisfied before leaving that they had found just the right place for their daughters. Around more than one hearth-stone's blazing fire was Miss Lyon described that cold Tuesday night; and more than one listening little girl, as she heard of the new-found teacher, wished she were older, that she too might be with Miss Lyon.

The school was opened on Wednesday morning at *nine o'clock,*—just as the young ladies had heard it would be; for punctuality then, as later, meant not half a minute from the appointed time. There were fifty pupils assembled in the old hall that morning, and the indications of home-sickness that were settling on some began to scatter, as they heard Miss Lyon say: "Now, young ladies, we shall feel very badly if you can't give us a part of your hearts. How many of you think your hearts are large enough to love, not only those good fathers and mothers and dear little brothers and sisters, but us also?" The old scholars' hands went straight up, and the new ones had so little control over theirs, that they were found almost at once in the same position. The teacher said: "I thought it was so;" and then, taking their hearts right into her heart, she asked God to bless them in all they should do that winter. Now they waited for directions in regard to their studies. And there came a more lasting than an April cloud over some of those countenances, when they heard that the new scholars would all be expected to study Colburn's First Lessons, Murray's Grammar, and perhaps Adams' Arithmetic, and Woodbridge's New Geography. The Colburn's Arithmetics were given out, and almost every eye saw, for its first question, " How many fingers have you on one hand?" What a feeling ran through those young hearts! If they could not speak, they could think, and it needed only Miss Lyon's discerning eye to read those thoughts: " Have I come here to count my fingers? It is too bad to spend fourteen dollars in this way. Oh, if I could only have known about this Colburn's Arithmetic before my father left!" But the fathers were all gone, and the teacher talked so cheerfully, and made every thing so pleasant, that they all recited their lesson with an outward grace, though the inner feeling was of being sacrificed to counting those fingers which they had learned to count while as yet they hardly knew the right hand from the left. The old scholars told the new ones that they were all the previous winter going through that arithmetic. Some believed, others doubted, while others still knew it *could not be so*. A few very conscientious ones felt called upon to make known the state of things to their parents. One, who longed to do it, did not think it best, because she saw that her father was perfectly delighted with Miss Lyon the day he brought her, and she thought he said to her: "My child may not know what it is best for her to study." There was nothing *she* could do; but perhaps the father of another might be influenced, and thus something be gained. So that other one wrote her father, counseled by her companions. In those days the mail went out from Buckland only three times a week, and, as no private opportunity occurred of sending, the letter was kept over Sunday. Miss Lyon made that day so pleasant, they were almost sorry they had written such a letter, and about concluded that, if they could be let off from Colburn's First Lessons, they would be willing to stay a little longer. But what should occur on Monday morning, but that Miss Lyon should go into school, and say: "Now, young ladies, I should not wonder if you felt as though you could not spend your time and money to learn to count your fingers, — that is, to study Colburn's First Lessons; neither would I wonder if you felt that your parents would not be willing to have you do it. But I rather think you had better not write those good fathers quite yet. I am afraid they will be very much troubled; and I really think you will find your powers a little more taxed than you now think for, in studying Colburn. Don't you think you had better try it for two weeks? and, if you want to leave it then, why, perhaps I shall think it is best for you to do it. Sometimes I change my mind, — sometimes my young ladies change their minds, and you may be very sure that I shall not want you to study Colburn's First Lessons if you don't want to do it." Oh, how ashamed were the letter-writers now! They longed for recess, and when it came, one whispered to the other: "She must have heard us talk Saturday." "No one can have told her, for we did not tell any one else." "She will think us so mean." "We will burn up the letter at once." It was consumed before recess closed, and those young ladies were in their seats, ready to do any thing, but wishing that Miss Lyon had not heard that Saturday's talk, of which, and of the letter, she really knew nothing till years afterward.

That was a happy winter for all those pupils. They can never forget their satisfaction in their arithmetic, nor how delighted Miss Lyon was when she found them ready to answer such questions as, "Four-fifths of fifteen are six-tenths of how many thirds of twenty-one?" as fast as she could read them; nor her greater delight in their explanations. Adams' Arithmetic became a new book under her teaching, and Woodbridge's Geography, with the geographical cards prepared by her, was "so interesting." And when she told them that "Grammar measures the whole mind," — and more, that "a young lady who can not go into grammar can not penetrate any thing," — they saw new beauties in it. They believed, with her, that it is "a great study," and that "a philosophical mind is required to understand the nature and foundation of language." And now they loved those Bible Lessons, made so pleasant from day to day. In their rooms they prepared their paper cards of the good old foolscap, and copied what Miss Lyon had made ready for them to help them in acquiring Scripture History. We do not know how many packages of cards there were, but we know there were twenty cards in a package, for we have often seen them in homes on the hills of Western Massachusetts, where children would interest themselves for hours, going over them. One perhaps would call out, "Sons of Noah?" — for this would appear on one side of the little card; then would come the answer, "Shem, Ham, and Japheth;" and perhaps the next would be, "Father and mother of Moses?" while the reply would be, "Amram and Jochebed." And yet another, "Sarah's age?" and the answer, "One hundred and twenty-seven." "Four rivers that watered Eden?" and a little, lisping girl would cry, "Pison, Gihon, Hiddekel, and Euphrates." How many mothers have thanked Miss Lyon for those Scripture cards on foolscap paper, not only for themselves but for their children!

Miss Lyon commenced that winter's work with hopes and fears, and saying: "I would not desire any thing, that would not be for the glory of God, and in accordance with the will of my Saviour." With the hope that her school might be visited by the Holy Spirit, and with the fear "that some might become so absorbed in their studies as to exclude God from their hearts," she prayed and labored to save the souls she tenderly loved. The last of December, she writes: "Some are thoughtful;" and adds: "That heart must be insensible which could not feel, in observing the general attention manifest when a sermon is reviewed, a Bible lesson recited, or any religious subject brought forward. Perhaps the Lord may visit us by his grace. In him is all our hope."

Tried in her own soul, she writes still further: "For a long time, I have at intervals been anxious about my own state of mind. I have felt that if I were ardently attached to the Saviour, my desires to honor him would be more uniform. I had hoped that the Lord would direct to means which would *effectually* move my soul, so that I could no longer sleep when reflecting on the cause of our dear Redeemer. But let me depend on nothing but God." There followed weeks of seriousness in that school, but no conversions. Miss Lyon's soul was stirred within her. She knew that the Spirit of God was in the midst of them, and that he was grieved. "And why," she asked, "should that Spirit be grieved from us, when he is so much more easily invited to stay with us, — to come and to bless us?"

Eleven pupils were hopefully pious at the beginning. Their souls were joined with hers in prayer; and when they feared that the Heavenly Dove was about to depart, the Lord came suddenly among them, and to abide with them by his converting grace. Those who witnessed the scenes of that closing term can understand her feelings as she wrote, a few weeks later: "Those days must be numbered with the most precious of my life; and sometimes I can scarcely believe that all those scenes were real." This was the first revival in a school of which Miss Lyon had the entire charge. Having wrestled with her God and prevailed, she wrote "Peniel" on that Buckland hall, — to come back, in after years, and find that her Saviour made it "Peniel" still; for we too had called it by that name.

Before that school-term closed, there was new joy in many of those homes from which daughters had gone forth on that cold Tuesday morning. In writing, a tender scene in one of those homes comes up vividly. A letter was handed to a father. He read and wept. It was given to the mother, and her tears flowed as soon as her eye fell upon the first line. The little children knew that the letter had come from Buckland. They looked on and were sad, not having yet learned that there are tears of joy as well as sorrow. "What is it, mamma?" said the eldest one. The letter was passed to the child and she read: "Your daughter has a trembling hope that she is a Christian. God is with us. Pray for us." Then the child wept with the parents, and there arose in her young heart the desire to know her sister's God, and she had no rest till she was numbered with the Lord's chosen ones.

Probably in as many as twenty of the homes of Western Massachusetts were there scenes like this during February and the early part of March, 1826. When the fathers went for their daughters, at the close of the term, they blessed Miss Lyon in God's name, and begged her to return to them the coming winter. The influence of those precious daughters, now Christ's, was not confined to their homes; it was felt also in their neighborhoods. Little prayer-meetings were commenced; new Sabbath-school teachers were to be found; benevolent societies for little children came into existence; pastors were encouraged, for they felt that there had been added to their numbers, not only those who should be saved, but also those who would seek to save others.

CHAPTER VI.

In Derry, Ashfield, and Buckland.

ALTERNATE LABORS IN DERRY AND ASHFIELD — PREPARING HER PUPILS TO BE TEACHERS — LETTERS TO MISS GRANT — NARRATIVE OF THE REVIVAL IN ASHFIELD SCHOOL — CLASSIFICATION OF THE PUPILS — HER SOLEMN APPEALS TO THE IMPENITENT — AND TO CHRISTIANS — IN IPSWICH — IN BUCKLAND IN 1829-30.

MISS LYON returned to Derry in the spring of 1826, to be once more with Miss Grant for the summer. Their school was again blessed; for during the first term twenty of the pupils hopefully became Christians. There were times when mothers of pupils in that school observed a concert of prayer on every Wednesday morning, between eight and nine o'clock, to offer their petitions that their daughters might there become Christ's. Miss Lyon's own mother, hearing of this, joined with those mothers in praying for their daughters. Those teachers alone, and perhaps not they, can tell how much they were strengthened by those mothers' prayers. The second term of this summer was also one of rich spiritual blessing.

The winter of 1826-7 was passed in Ashfield and in the old Sanderson's Academy. A goodly number of young ladies were again assembled, and Miss Lyon, with heart and hands full, thanked God every day for so much to do. She gave more attention than before to the external deportment of her pupils. Some who were then with her can never forget her manner of saying: "Young ladies should always speak with a gentle voice. Gentleness and sprightliness can walk hand in hand. Come to see me with a quiet footstep. I shall not care to know of your approach till you knock at my door."

New studies were introduced into this school, for her pupils were becoming more advanced, and they were charged to seek to have their minds act with vigor and activity. The "power of abstraction" was a prominent topic in the talks of that winter; and it was so acted upon that some really thought they were able to do a three hours' work in one hour. Young ladies desiring to teach had now begun to resort to the school; and before the term closed, most of the pupils had engaged schools on the hills for the summer. Miss Lyon's words of counsel to such were not few, nor were they ill-chosen. She would say to them: "Young ladies, just think what a privilege it is to labor for immortal minds. How much better than to spend your lives seeking happiness alone! The life that I desire for you is as much above the pleasure-seeker's as an archangel is above an infant. You have been accustomed to follow where I have led you. Now you are to be seated on a throne of your own. You can sway a golden scepter there. Be sure to dc it." For those who were not to teach, she had also kind words. She pointed them to the homes they were to bless, the mothers they were to comfort, to the fathers of whom it is truly said: "The daughters shall lead them." She bade them continue to seek mental improvement, saying: "You can do this, and still be good business characters. Versatility is given you for this purpose; and I hope I shall hear that you make your mothers' cares your cares."

When those pupils had really gone to their homes, Miss Lyon wrote Miss Grant: "The demand from our common schools is so urgent, that I feel it to be a duty to endeavor to do something at least *one winter* more. I have therefore made engagements to return here next autumn." After a summer with Miss Grant in Derry, she was again found in Ashfield, with fifty pupils around her. She says of them: "Our school is uncommonly good, — several degrees better than the school last year." It was Miss Lyon's happiness to be always favored with "the best" at the present time. She was never mourning over some past good taken from her, but enjoying present good, doing present work, and impressing upon her pupils that "the duty of the present moment is of more consequence than all future duty. We never heard her say: "I am disappointed in my school;" and she rarely said: "I am disappointed in this young lady." In later years she was accustomed to say to her school: "I usually find young ladies worth a great deal more than I expected. Where I am once disappointed for the worse, I am ten times for the better." And could those young ladies, who heard her thus speak, have passed behind the curtain, where she communed with her teachers alone, they would have found the same kindness. One of those teachers wrote a widowed mother: "Give your sensitive E. to Miss Lyon, who is all kindness. I found her kind when I was her pupil, but now that I am a teacher, and hear her speak *of* her pupils, I realize that she is unlike any one I ever knew. She said to us yesterday in our teachers' meeting: 'Do for and speak of these young ladies, just as you would wish us to do for your own dear sister. They are our daughters, — our sisters. We must never speak lightly of them. We must remember that we have in them a most precious trust.'" These words were penned years after Mt. Holyoke Seminary was in successful operation, but the spirit was the same when Miss Lyon was in Ashfield and Buckland.

The group that gathered around her in December, 1827, shared largely in her interest. She saw in them the teachers of the summer schools of that region.

She knew that "committee-men" had been chosen in November, instead of March as had been customary, that they might be ready to take as teachers the first, best fruits of her school. She knew that what she did was to be done over many times, in the old brown and the new red school-houses of the hills, when she had gone to Ipswich for the summer. Pupils and teacher had a mind to work, and Miss Lyon says: "There was delightful progress in study;" but she was not satisfied with this alone. She felt that those immortal spirits would be satisfied only in knowing and loving God. She asked this for them; and, when alone, she reviewed her own life as a Christian, and mourned over it. Her own words best give her feelings in that review: "What an immense loss I must suffer through life, on account of the misimprovement of so long a period of my existence! I humbly hope I shall finally be saved, although as by fire; but I have no reason to expect ever in this world all that spiritual enjoyment with which I might have been favored, if all these years had witnessed a regular advance in a life of faith and piety. Neither can I expect that satisfaction and success in laboring in the cause of the Saviour which I might have enjoyed, if I had received that preparation which can be gained by no means but by a long course of active, faithful obedience."

She particularly felt that she had not done all that

she should have done for Christians, and says of it: "During all these years, I know not how many just commencing a life of godliness may have received an impression from me which will be felt all their lives. May I, in this, be saved from blood-guiltiness. But I tremble lest even this winter should bear witness against me. Almost half of my pupils have more or less hope that they are friends of the Redeemer. Several have indulged this hope but a few months; in some it is like the faint glimmering of a distant taper. But few can be considered established Christians; and of scarcely any have I much evidence that they possess deep feeling and lively faith. Here we are: what shall we do? what can we do? The influence of these on each other, the influence from absorbing studies, and that which I may exert, may produce an impression which shall effect their whole lives. These precious souls have been sent here by the providence of God; but what to do I know not. I am weaker than weakness itself, and my wisdom is altogether folly. May I be more and more sensible of the preciousness of the direction, — 'If any of you lack wisdom, let him ask of God.'"

The above was written to Miss Grant, Jan. 6th, 1828, and probably to no other one would she have opened her heart thus freely. To the same friend she writes Feb. 25th, when God was beginning to turn their captivity: "Before my last letter to you, I thought I had reason to believe that the Spirit of God was finding a resting-place in the hearts of some professors of religion in school. I did hope, too, that there was a secret, silent influence on the minds of some of the impenitent. This continued to increase till not a doubt remained that the Lord was indeed among us. Since last Friday morning, our school-room has been a solemn place. During these five days, four have had a change of feeling, which has led them to hope they have passed from death unto life. About a week before, there was one instance of hopeful conversion. Several are now deeply anxious; some are inquiring with interest, and I know of only *one* entirely unaffected. I tell you all, for we need your prayers. Our state is most critical. I do not feel it to be the time for rejoicing, but for mourning, solemnity, and deep humiliation before God. I fear, first, lest *I* shall grieve the Spirit; and then I fear for the friends of the Redeemer here."

The following letter, written after the term closed, gives a fuller account of the work of grace enjoyed in the school that winter:—

"ASHFIELD, March 18, 1828.

"I have this day parted with my dear pupils. Since I last wrote you, my labors have been greatly increased ; but that they have been thus increased, I consider one of the greatest blessings I have ever enjoyed.

"When our school commenced, I had a faint hope that the Lord would visit us by his Holy Spirit. But, on viewing my own heart, I felt that I had very little reason to expect it. There I found an apathy, chilling and distressing. It seemed almost as if the fallow ground could not be broken up. I felt that I was taking on myself a great responsibility; but what to do I scarcely knew; and the little that I did know I was very poorly prepared to perform.

"The first week, I made a separation in the school after the plan that you have generally practiced. To my surprise, nearly twenty were found, who, in some form or other, indulged a hope that they were the friends of God. This affected my heart. The responsibility of attempting to do something for their spiritual improvement rested on my mind with an indescribable weight. It seemed to me that something must be done; but I felt that I could do little more than endeavor to ascertain something about them individually, and attempt to commit them to God. . . .

"For several weeks, my desires for the impenitent were faint and few; and almost all I met, either in school or out, appeared to partake of the same spirit. I used to say to Miss W., that if the Lord should visit this school, we must always remember it as one of the more wonderful displays of his power, which he sometimes condescends to make. We would recount the scenes of Buckland, and contrast some, who, from the commencement of the term there, seemed to pray the prayer of faith, with those in this school who were the most interested for the salvation of souls; and we would say, 'There is no prospect of a revival, for this is not the way that God generally works;' and then my heart would sink within me. Thus I lived on, week after week, till more than half the term was gone. But while man looketh on the outward appearance, God judgeth righteous judgment. I now believe that the eye, which saw seven thousand in Israel who had not bowed the knee to Baal, has seen the effectual prayer rising continually from some hearts in towns around us, though I knew it not at the time.

"The eighth week of the school, Rev. Mr. M., of H., called to take a daughter home on account of sickness in the family. A friend of mine, who is himself a clergyman, has remarked to me that he considered it no disparagement to any of his ministerial brethren in this region to say that he should prefer Mr. M. for *his* minister; though he can not be said to excel in preaching. At the time he came for his daughter, I saw him only a moment. After expressing a great interest in the school, on account of its influence on society, and on accouut of its containing so many teachers for district schools the ensuing summer, he said that he had been anxious for its *spiritual* prosperity. *He only said it;* but it found a resting-place in my heart, and there it has rested to the present time. I could read, in his countenance and manner, that it was not an expression of common interest. It seemed suited at once to encourage and reprove me, and also to humble me in the dust. I have since learned, in more ways than one, that he has undoubtedly had great anxiety for souls here; and I believe some others have had a like spirit. It is worthy of notice that the attention commenced among the young ladies from Mr. M.'s parish, and was almost entirely confined to them for some time. It did seem that the prayers of this good man were answered. He has since said to me, that he had indeed been anxious for the school; but in the ardent desires of his heart, he had not been conscious of making any selection, even though he had a daughter here without God and without hope.

"This daughter returned after an absence of three weeks; but her father said he did not bring her, depending on the school to give her a new heart. She found the influences in her room entirely changed. Her three companions, young ladies from the same town, were all rejoicing in hope. They had been ardently desiring her return, and now they could not see her willing to reject the Saviour. She was immediately affected ; but I did not dare to hope, for a while, that it was any thing but sympathy. Soon, however, her tears were exchanged for a solemn and distressed countenance, which bespoke deep, heartfelt sorrow. For a few days, her distress was great. Though generally very much inclined to converse, she would now pass the whole morning without scarcely speaking a word; and her companions, though possessing all the joy and ardor of young converts, were awed into silence; and, like Job's friends, 'none spake a word.' In eight days after her return, she was brought to rejoice in hope of a blessed immortality.

"During the whole winter, Scripture recitations have been uncommonly impressive, compared with the means used to make them so. This interest was most manifest when the subject was a solemn one, such as 'the mercy seat;' 'the thunderings of Mount Sinai,' &c. During some of these still and impressive exercises, it did seem that the effect must remain; but the first recess would carry it all away. It was not until about the middle of the term that I became sensible that professing Christians were more awake, and felt more deeply their responsibility. Sometimes we hoped that the mind of here and there one among the impenitent was not quite so indifferent as usual. The first of the tenth week I was convinced that the Holy

Spirit was indeed among us. From this time, with a very few apparent interruptions, the work went forward with a regular and increasing advance, till the very last day. About twenty expressed hope in the Saviour, six or seven left without hope, of whom two were not deeply affected. One of them tried to be interested, depending on her own efforts ; but her efforts were in vain.

"The work was very still ; so much so that many in town knew scarcely any thing about it. Our school exercises were as usual. Many of our friends, who visited us, observed nothing to mark this as the place where the Spirit was operating so powerfully, except a general stillness, and here and there a deeply solemn countenance. But to us connected with the school the work has appeared great and wonderful. We have daily said to each other, 'Can this be true?' It has been carried on so independently of means, that we have frequently felt that our best hopes might easily be blasted ; and as frequently that the Lord could work and none could hinder. We have all had the conviction daily that this work is wholly of the Lord. The effect of this revival on those who indulged a hope at the commencement of the school has been favorable. Many of them seemed to leave the school with a much higher sense of their obligation to labor continually for the kingdom of Christ."

In this letter Miss Lyon speaks of " a separation in the school." By this she means that the pupils were requested to class themselves among the friends of God, or otherwise, according to their own convictions of their state. When this was done, there were meetings once a week for each class, and instructions given suited to their need. She had first seen this practiced in a school by Mr. Emerson in Byfield, and subsequently by Miss Grant in her schools. This was probably the first time she had done it herself, but she always looked back upon this winter as one in which she was specially led of God, and ever after practiced this course in her own schools.

This classification was usually called for at a devotional exercise in the opening of the term, and will never be forgotten by any who were asked to decide to which class they belonged. We can even now, after the lapse of years, see her loving eye resting upon us after the names had been taken of those who had professed Christ publicly; of those who had not done this, but still had some hope in him; then of those who had no hope. We hear her say: " This should remind us of the last great day of separation. If death should come to us to-night, would the separation be the same as this now made? Is it not almost certain that some whose names are written as Christians, if called away, would hear the fearful words, 'I never knew you.' Are there not many whose names are written without hope who desire to begin to love the Saviour here? Are not the prayers of pious parents in heaven and on earth to be answered in these names being entered in the Book of Life?" Those were solemn moments to us all, when Miss Lyon thus spoke, and the prayers that followed led not a few to feel, as never before, that we live for eternity.

In her letter to Miss G. she also speaks of Scripture recitations, — of the mercy-seat, — the thunderings of Mount Sinai. No pupil could dwell on that mercy-seat of pure gold with Miss Lyon, and not receive a deep impression; fixing it distinctly in mind that the length thereof was two cubits and a half, and a cubit and a half the breadth thereof; and making us to see a cherub on the one end, and a cherub on the other end, she would add, with deepest reverence: "Now hear God say, 'There I will meet thee, and commune with thee from above the mercy-seat.' Yes, there, from off that mercy-seat, the shadow of a good thing to come, even of Him who is now in the presence of God for us, we hear Jehovah speak. He speaks of mercy, — of peace; but with that broken law honored, yes, guarded well in the holy ark of the covenant, and under the shadow of that blessed mercy-seat, the type of Him who covereth our sins. The faces of the cherubim are toward the mercy-seat, and thus the holy angels 'desire to look into' that 'way into the holiest' of all, where we may obtain eternal redemption. Shall we refuse what angels desire to know?"

Nor was the lesson from Exodus xix. less impressive, as she would call us to hear God say to Israel: "If ye will obey my voice indeed and keep my covenant, then ye shall be a peculiar treasure to me above all people." Then she would bid us think of that great multitude, — three millions at least, — their voices resounding like waves, saying "all that the Lord hath spoken, we will do." "This was a striking manifestation to them when they had not the Bible; the influences of the Spirit were then mightily felt. There were many circum stances that combined to give overpowering solemnity: they were not to come near; to wait for three days; the lightnings and thunderings that made them quake as they stood at the foot of the mount, and looked up to see it rising to heaven; the sound of that trumpet, as if blown by God himself; the unearthly stillness of all else; Sinai on smoke. Is it not a fearful thing to break a law thus given? But, beloved, you are spoken to, not from Mount Sinai, but from Mount Zion. Jesus speaks. See that ye refuse not him who speaketh from heaven, and who would give you a kingdom, which can not be moved. If you will not do it, you shall realize that 'our God is a consuming fire.'"

Such were some of those "still impressive exercises," in which the whole school shared from day to day. We know that Miss Lyon labored most successfully for Christians through that winter, though she hardly dared to think it was so at the time. That season of blessing led her to feel that in trying to benefit Christians, she was especially laboring *with* Christ, because of the love he bears to those whom he has redeemed. She studied the epistles of Paul with new interest, and found that it was Christians of whom he "always" and "without ceasing" made mention in his prayers, and for whom he thanked God on every remembrance, even on every mention of their names. She realized that it was not the impenitent alone that were the burden of his heart, but that there came on him also and daily too "the care of all the churches." His practical instructions were made hers, as she met Christians from week to week. She did not ask to have them removed from the world, but that they might be kept from the evil in the world, by being clothed upon with Christ. As she thus prayed, always jealous of her own heart, and thus labored for Christians and the impenitent, and brought others to labor also, ever looking up and saying, "All my springs are in Thee," should we not expect to see greater things than these? Shall we wonder that the next year, 1829, she thus speaks in February of the work in her school at Buckland: "I can not describe the scenes I have witnessed. It is the Lord's doing, and it is marvelous in our eyes. The rapidity with which this work of grace has been carried forward the week past has never been equaled, I think, where I have been permitted to be an eye-witness." There were fifteen then sealed for Christ in one week in her school of seventy-four pupils. During that winter, Miss Lyon was suffering from a severe family affliction, and she has told us that, when she carried her own personal trials to Christ, she found it easier than at any other time to speak with him of her dear school.

"Trials made the promise sweet;
Trials gave new life to prayer."

The following summer found her in Ipswich, with Miss Grant, laboring in a revival which she says was "silent and gradual, but the effects certain." While many remained unaffected, there were at least fifteen precious souls, as was believed, sealed for eternal life. She said of this: "When I can realize a little of the value of one soul, I feel that a great work has been accomplished; but when I remember, that Jesus died for *all* our pupils, I can but ask, why did not *all* hear his voice? Did my unbelief prevent it?"

Miss Lyon passed the winter of 1829-30 in Buckland. It was understood that she would no more come into those parts, to abide even for a single season.

The good people of the place made every effort to accommodate boarders, one of them saying: "Bring all who will come. We will board them all, if necessary, for nothing." When no other place could be found, this gentleman gave up a large room in the attic of his house, which was divided into four apartments by suspending bedquilts and blankets, and was occupied by eight persons. He received twenty-four into his family; and, while the wife was sometimes inclined to doubt whether they derived any pecuniary benefit from such boarders, he was more than satisfied with the arrangement when he saw his boys stimulated to greater exertion in their studies by them, and when, after the revival commenced, he heard the low murmur of prayer coming from every room in his house.

The school, which six winters before had only twenty-five pupils, now numbered ninety-nine. Miss Lyon found her labors abundant and "cares almost overwhelming." But she "never had so good a school, never saw young ladies love to study so well, and never more docile." She had herself enjoyed much when studying, but said this winter: "Much as I value an education, I value such a field of labor as this more. Who am I, that so many parents should be willing to trust their daughters to me; and what was my father's house, that my God should give me such blessed work from year to year?" Early in the term she saw indications for good in the tenderness of some of the impenitent, and felt that some Christians were pleading earnestly for the salvation of souls. In January, she began to fear that the *great* blessing was to be denied; but before February had passed, she writes: "It does seem as if we had nothing to do this week but to stand still and see the salvation of God." "The school is very solemn, and marked by a deep and pervading stillness." The results of that winter's labors are best told in the following letter to a sister, written a week after the term closed: —

"I should be glad to give you a description of this school; but it would be impossible. I believe that my schools here have been more and more interesting every winter; and we all think this has been most so of all. I have never witnessed such an improvement in moral character, in ardent desire to possess meekness, humility, patience, perseverance, &c. A spirit of benevolence has seemed to reign among us to such a degree that selfishness has appeared to most of our little community somewhat in its own character. We have made it an object to gain enlarged and correct views, especially relating to our own country, its present state, its interesting character, its wants, its prospects, as to what needs to be done, what can be done, what ought to be done, and, finally, as to what is our duty. Many intelligent, refined young ladies, who have been brought up in the lap of indulgence, thought they should be willing to go to the remotest corner of the world, and teach a school among the most degraded and ignorant, might it only be said of them by their Master as it was said of one of old, 'She hath done what she could.' But more than all, we have been visited by the influence of the Holy Spirit. Soon after the commencement of the school, the gentle dews began to descend and continued to increase until the last week, when we were blessed with a plentiful and refreshing shower. More than thirty expressed some hope that they had found the Saviour precious to their souls. At the commencement of the term more than forty indulged this hope. Among these there was evidently great improvement in Christian character. It has seemed as if the effects of this work of the Spirit must continue."

And they did continue. Miss Lyon often remarked: "How easy it is to work *with* the Holy Spirit!" It was easy for her, because she was, as it were, one with that Spirit. Those closing days in Buckland she worked "with the Spirit;" and, feeling that she was doing her last work for many, her mind and heart wrought with a power almost divine. Mrs. Cowles, who knew her well, has said: "In seasons of the most intimate communion, her words were often apples of gold which one could wish to preserve in pictures of silver. Nothing but pearls and diamonds fell from her lips." One of those Buckland pupils has furnished us with a few of those precious words which fell from her lips when they were sorrowing lest they should see her face no more. She says: "Miss Lyon has said to us many times during the winter: 'What you will do in the world may depend very much on the way you spend your time here.' And when that time was spent and we were about to go forth, as we listened to her words, we felt that through her we were hearing a voice from heaven. We can never forget her earnestness as she said: 'Now I trust you will be inflexible in regard to *the right*. Do not yield that, even to please kings; but be very careful to distinguish between the right and personal gratification.' 'Make all you can of your intellectual and moral powers and of your influence over others.' 'Do something; have a plan; live for some purpose; be faithful and conscientious and understand what you are to do; but do not expect to make over this world, or to greatly change your condition in it; but seek, rather, to be ready to do and to bear what comes in your way. Be willing to do any thing any where that Providence seems to lay upon you.' 'Do not expect to be independent because educated. Ladies never can be independent; and those best educated most feel their dependence. They must expect great demands to be made upon their time and strength; and they should meet them in the spirit of Him who came to minister, rather than to be ministered unto. You will find no pleasure like the pleasure of active effort. May God give every one of you more and more for your heart and hands to do, and more and more fellowship with Christ in his sufferings. Never be hasty to decide that you can not do, because you have not physical or mental strength. Never say you have no faith or hope. Always think of God's strength when you feel your weakness, and remember that you can come nearer to him than to any being in the universe. We have desired to educate you to go among the rich or the poor, to live in the country or the village, in New England, the West, or in a foreign land. And, wherever you are, remember that God will be with you, if you seek to do good to immortal souls.' "

The traces of the beneficial influence of these schools may still be seen strongly impressed on all the hill towns about Buckland and Ashfield. Eternity alone can disclose what those pupils have done for immortal souls. Many remember how they labored, in the spirit and with the Spirit, in the revivals of 1830-31, which so soon followed. Many young hearts had seen in them that there is a beauty in holiness; and many an Elijah heard from them that there is a little cloud, even as a man's hand, rising in the distance. The Elijahs could be sure that they would watch the spreading cloud; and, when there was abundance of rain, so that plants of righteousness were springing up on every side, they knew that, like her at whose feet they had sat, they would watch carefully to see that not a leaf or twig of the tender plants was turned out of its place.

We find the value of Miss Lyon's labors already so fully appreciated, that Mr. Griswold, who had so generously welcomed her and her scholars to his house at the commencement of this term, proposed to combine with others in erecting a large building in Buckland for her school, that it might be permanently established there; but the Lord's time had not come. His instrument was not yet fully fitted for her work.

CHAPTER VII.

Founding of Mount Holyoke Seminary.

FOUR YEARS AT IPSWICH — EDUCATING THE FUTURE MOTHERS OF AMERICA — DESIRE FOR A PERMANENT INSTITUTION FOR FEMALE EDUCATION — SELF-CONSECRATION TO THIS OBJECT — THE CORNER-STONE LAID — FRIENDS AND HELPERS — NAMES OF THE FOUNDERS GRATEFULLY CHERISHED — UNWEARIED LABORS — DR. HITCHCOCK'S TESTIMONY.

FOR four years after leaving Buckland, Miss Lyon was associated with Miss Grant in Ipswich. There they were richly blessed in labor, and many souls were brought to Christ. There they enjoyed some seasons of very marked outpourings of the Spirit. One year they could say: "There is seldom a time when some one belonging to the seminary is not apparently seeking the way of eternal life." They saw pupils go forth to bless homes and to bless the world, and their hearts rejoiced. They thanked the Lord that they could prepare teachers; and, in speaking of seeing young ladies who had gone from them, in their own homes, Miss Lyon says: "I have realized more than ever before that my field of labor was among the most desirable. I have thanked God, who has given me this work to do. Oh, how immensely important is the preparation of the daughters of the land to be good mothers! If they are prepared for this situation, they will have the most important preparation which they can have for any other. While, in the good providence of God, I have been permitted to occupy a field of labor where I could aid in preparing some who must mold the char acter of future generations for their great work, and while I have enjoyed much in my labor, I have not been quite satisfied." Thus she wrote her mother in 1834, feeling, as when a child, that in every step she must have her mother's approval. She was not satisfied; for from her quiet scene of labor she looked out upon a world. She did not talk of woman's rights, and said little of woman's sphere; but she did love to dwell on the great work God has given woman to do; and she was convinced that to do that work well she must be educated.

Miss Lyon was often heard to say: "It does seem to me a less evil that farmers and mechanics have scanty stores of knowledge, such as our common schools give, than that their wives, the mothers of their children, should be uneducated." She longed to see woman's mind better trained; to see the public feeling that it must be so, and making as liberal provision for the education of their daughters as of their sons. She believed that there must be permanent seminaries for young ladies, under boards of trustees, to secure the best literary and religious advantages, and to give the public confidence that the advantages of a good school would not pass away with teachers then on the stage. About this time, good Mr. Emerson was called to heaven. As she saw the chariot of God bear him above, and received his falling mantle, she asked more earnestly than ever before that a house might be built to his God, whither American daughters might go up, till the end of time, to be educated for high and holy service on earth, and whose works should follow them when they should rest from labors here.

Her own words give her ideas of permanency: "The permanency of an institution is found in its perpetual vitality and in its continued prosperity and usefulness. The first is to be secured in the same manner that the principle of perpetual life in our higher institutions for young men has been so effectually preserved. A fund is to be committed to an independent, self-perpetuating board of trustees, known to the churches as faithful, responsible men; not as a proprietary investment, but as a free offering, leaving them no way for an honorable retreat from their trust, and binding them with solemn responsibilities to hundreds and thousands of donors, who have committed their sacred charities to their conscientious fidelity.

Most of our distinguished female seminaries have no principle of perpetual life. Amidst all their prosperity, they have no solid foundation, and, in themselves, no sure principle of continued existence Could we secure to our public institutions the continued labors of the same teachers, through an antediluvian life, the preservation of the vital principle would be a subject of much less consequence. But in view of the present shortened life of man, and in view of the many changes which are breaking in upon the continued services of those to whose care these institutions are committed, every reflecting mind must regard it as of the very first importance to secure this principle."

George W. Heard, Esq., of Ipswich, whose name and encouragement in the work Miss Lyon always gratefully remembered, says of her at this time: "Plans for founding a permanent seminary engaged her thoughts early and late, and, I might almost say, unceasingly." He saw her "reliant trust in Providence," and cheerfully helped one whom God was using in so noble a cause. Miss Lyon saw very great difficulties to be overcome in founding such an institution, but she said: "I do believe such a work will be effected at some future day, perhaps some twenty or fifty years from this time." As she withdrew from Ipswich, in the autumn of 1834, to give herself wholly to the noble cause, she said: "I never had a prospect of engaging in any labor, which seemed so directly the work of the Lord as this. It is very sweet, in the midst of darkness and doubt, to commit the whole to his guidance." But she adds: "I am about to embark in a frail boat on a boisterous sea. I know not whither I shall be driven, nor how I shall be tossed, nor to what port I shall be directed." It is true that she was in a frail bark and on an unexplored, as well as boisterous sea; for as yet there was no such seminary as she proposed in our land or world. But the cause was committed to One who knew every shoal, breaker, and circling eddy of that sea. Rich in the choicest pilots, he gave some to go forth with her in the first launching of the frail boat; and when, upon the deep sea, the waves seemed ready to swallow it up, he had in reserve others with no less skill to go to her aid. And so, after two years of tossings and calling unto God from the depths, we find that there came a day in which he stilled the waves and the billows, and "commanded his loving-kindness," and that day was Oct. 3d, 1836, when those friends came together and laid the corner-stone of Mt. Holyoke Seminary. Miss Lyon then wrote: "And I have indeed lived to see the time when a body of gentlemen have ventured to lay the corner-stone of an edifice which will cost about $15,000, and will be an institution for the education of females." Upon that corner-stone she stooped down and wrote: "The Lord hath remembered our low estate," and felt that another stone in the foundation of our great system of benevolent operations, which are destined, in the hand of God, to convert the world, had been laid.

She said of the prospective seminary: "Had I a thousand lives, I could sacrifice them all in suffering and hardship for its sake. Did I possess the greatest fortune, I could readily relinquish it all, and become poor and more than poor, if its prosperity should demand it." She thanked God for the privilege of doing, saying: "The feeble efforts which I am permitted to put forth in coöperating with others in laying the foundation of this new seminary will probably do more for the cause of Christ, after I am laid in my grave, than all I have done in my life before."

Miss Lyon went forth to her work committing it to God. If ever one prayed "without ceasing" she did. She knew how to come to God, for she believed that "he is, and that he is a rewarder of them that diligently seek him." She has told us that from a child, she never knew what it was to be skeptical. She could no more doubt God's existence than her own. She had known what it was to go to an earthly father with all the desires of her young heart; and she fully believed that her heavenly Father was as ready to hear her, if she was as ready to trust him. And now, assured that she was doing God's work, she carried every thing to him. She expected to meet trials as she went on, and she says she never asked to be free from them; she only desired God's will to be done. She longed for the sympathy of friends in the work; but she has told us that she became willing to labor, if there were only a very few to go with her. But friends were given her and her cause. Once, when fearing that she had grieved one who had been aiding her, she retired to her chamber to plead with God that that friend's interest might still be given to the dear seminary, willing to lose it herself, if her Father saw that to be necessary. She loved to trace that Father's hand in providing each of these friends. Her book of Providence was a very large one, and it was a rich feast to sit by her side, have her open page after page, and hear her read those parts where "Providence" was inscribed on the left-hand page, and "Friends of the Seminary" on the right-hand. Mr. Choate of Essex tells us how gently he and others in Eastern Massachusetts tried to rock the cradle of Mt. Holyoke Seminary, and how, at Miss Lyon's bidding, they endeavored carefully to carry it in their arms. Miss Lyon has told us how that band of noble men did rock that cradle till it found a resting-place in South Hadley. She would say: "I want every one of my pupils to know the names of Dana, Felt, Choate, Heard, and Packard. We owe them much. They were our friends when our cause had hardly taken a place among the good objects of our day. Upon the one thousand dollars * given by the Ipswich ladies, for the seminary, she looked very much as she did upon the first money given her by her brother. She could seldom speak of those friends without a moistened eye, and her early Holyoke pupils were not slow to make their names household words, as well as the names of all those who were numbered among the patrons and guardians of the seminary while it was yet in its infancy. One of the early pupils says: "I had been hardly a week in South Hadley before I had heard of all those early friends of the seminary from Miss Lyon's lips. She had so told us of Dr. Humphrey and Dr. Hitchcock, that the very mention of their names filled us with reverence. We had heard of the faithfulness of Mr. Tyler and Mr. Bowdoin, and were assured that Deacon Safford, Deacon Porter, and Deacon Avery would soon come to see us. And when they came, their kind interest showed us that their heart was even as Miss Lyon's heart. We saw that they needed not the Pauline injunction: 'Help those women that labored with me in the

* This was the first donation made toward the seminary, and was often spoken of by Miss Lyon as its corner-stone.

Lord.'" Miss Lyon had said, in 1834, that those who should first put a hand to this work, saying to others, "Come and do likewise," would "deserve a place with Mills and Robert Raikes, and others of like eminence." We would join their names with Miss Lyon's in what one has said of her, and repeat: "Oh! what a glorious gate to heaven they were permitted to rear. And as, age after age, the long procession of redeemed ones shall pass through into the kingdom, and each shall add a star to their crowns, what a reward will they eternally be reaping!" Their names are reverenced on earth, and we are confident that our God has written them among those whose works shall follow them, not only to heaven, but through all eternity. They not only saw that corner-stone laid, and sympathized most tenderly with Miss Lyon as she wept tears of joy over the fallow ground now broken up, but, as they saw those rising walls, they could say with her: "The stones and brick and mortar speak a language which vibrates through the very soul." They prayed with her that the walls of the new seminary might be salvation, its gates praise, and "that no wicked hand might ever be allowed to turn it aside from its consecration to the Redeemer."

It was more than a year after the laying of that corner-stone, before the seminary was opened for the reception of pupils, and Miss Lyon felt that she had again, to use her own words, "a footing sufficiently firm for her feet to rest upon for the remainder of her days, and where her hands could work" for young ladies, who, she hoped would live for Christ. No human pen can record the labors of that year. At one time she was by Dea. Porter's side, watching the growing edifice; at another making arrangements for furnishing the seminary, by writing letters and circulars. She accompanied Mr. Hawkes, as he went from town to town to solicit funds, — a work which she once said, "cost me more trial of feeling than any thing I ever did, because I knew that my reasons for doing it were not understood." But she added with a smile: "Perhaps I should not have sufficiently valued the precious opportunity for laboring, that is now mine, had I not passed through just this trial." But with all this labor and trial, she found many bright spots in the pilgrimage and toils of that year. One was "a very interesting little meeting in Dea. Safford's parlor," in Boston, at the close of which a subscription of more than three thousand dollars was taken up for the new seminary. As she used to dwell on that meeting, she would tell us how Mr. Stoddard, of Boston, first said to her, "Dea. Safford is just the man to carry forward this work" for you; and how, while she was praying over it, yet another friend had said the same to her; and then how, in course of time, she received letters from Dea. Safford, that led her to his house. And she would say: "I can not describe my feelings as I found myself really at his door. Between the ringing of the door-bell and the response, I tried to roll all my care upon the Lord, and to be willing to receive not one encouraging word, if so my God might be most honored. But he was better to me than my fears. I found, in Mr. and Mrs. Safford, hearts all ready to enter into my plans. God had prepared those hearts." And at this point, she would perhaps be able to go no further, only adding: "How faithful is our God!" But another day would find her asking you to sit close by her, while she should tell you a little of her first visit in Monson, when Dea. Porter was secured for the dear seminary. She never forgot to tell the one listening to her, that she did not find Mr. Porter at home when she first went to his house, and that she had two days of prayer, and of seeking to be willing to give up the counsels and aid of the man who seemed so very desirable, before she could even talk with him. And she would add: "And now don't you think God has given us, in Mr. Porter, the very best man his storehouse could furnish?"

With delight we learned those lessons of truth and submission from Miss Lyon, with their fruits before us in the seminary. She used to say more impressively than any one to whom we ever listened: "Experience has taught me to fear the gratification of any ardent desire, unless I first feel a perfect willingness to yield my will entirely." In the yielding of that will, Providence gave her some of the choicest spirits on earth to help her build a house to the Lord. Some of these had known her in early years, while others had become links in the golden chain of friends of a later period. They were all loved by her, and esteemed very highly for their work's sake. Perhaps the estimate of these friends of hers can not better be expressed than in the words of Dr. Hitchcock, of Amherst, at the recent quarter-century celebration of Mt. Holyoke Seminary. After alluding to her being in his family when he was a pastor in Conway more than forty years before, as well as at later periods, he says: "And then how often have I met her in a great variety of circumstances in subsequent years! Yet I feel constrained to testify, what I could of only one or two human beings, that, in all this intercourse, I can not recall any thing morally wrong in her words or actions, nor unkind or ungenerous feeling toward any human being, although often sorely provoked by their treatment of her. I do not mean that Miss Lyon had attained to Christian perfection; but, were any one to assert that such a grace was hers, I confess that my memory could bring no facts to refute the claim."

But we must not dwell longer on those friends, who

were given to found Mt. Holyoke Seminary, and who, to use Miss Lyon's own words, "were raised up and brought into the field just when and where they were needed, and were continually receiving fresh anointings from the Lord for the holy service."

CHAPTER VIII.

The First Year.

THE OPENING OF THE SEMINARY — RECITATIONS — EDWARDS' HISTORY OF REDEMPTION — BIBLE LESSONS — RELIGIOUS EXERCISES — MISS LYON'S BIBLE AND HYMN BOOK — WEEKLY RELIGIOUS MEETINGS — THE HOUSE-KEEPING DEPARTMENT — JOY IN SUCCESS — THE FIRST ANNIVERSARY — MISS LYON'S MANNER ON ANNIVERSARY OCCASIONS.

NOV. 8, 1837, was the day fixed for the opening of Mt. Holyoke Seminary. Sept. 14th, of the same year, Miss Lyon had written to Miss Grant: "When I look through to Nov. 8, it seems like looking down a precipice of many hundred feet, which I must descend. I can only avoid looking at the bottom, and fix my eye on the nearest stone, till I have safely reached it." With the eye fixed on Him who cared for her, she went forward; and, on the appointed day, she had her eighty young ladies with her, as of old, thankful for such a precious charge, and sad in the thought that she had been obliged to refuse other eighties, because there was no place for them in the house that had been builded to the Lord. It is not strange that she was not at rest till able to lengthen the cords of her tabernacle, while so many were left without; and indeed the pattern first shown her in the Mount provided for two hundred and fifty, rather than eighty. But as the offerings of God's people were not sufficient for this, she said: "We will begin, and when it shall be seen what is the manner of our building, and the ordinances of our house, may be the wise-hearted will give us of their treasures till we can finish building the house of the Lord."

Perhaps Miss Lyon never more endeared herself to any pupils than those of the first year. Their zeal for the prosperity of the new seminary was hardly less than her own. They loved it all the more for the sacrifices they were called to make, — for sharing her toils. They can never forget her manner, as she said: "Every brick of this house is sacred to the Lord. All the money given to it was consecrated by prayer. I look upon all as just as sacred as if the means had been drawn directly from our missionary treasuries. The founders of this institution expect (and they have a right to expect it) that it will be a fountain of good to the world; that the cause of Christ will be advanced by the influences that go forth from it.

"You must not call this Miss Lyon's school. I regard it so much a child of Providence, that I do not like to have my name made prominent. And you would look upon it much as I do, if you could see a few of the many gulfs, that were to me impassable, made passable by a divine hand. All has sometimes seemed to hang upon some slight pivot, without which the whole would have fallen to the ground. I can see a ruling Hand in every thing connected with its establishment; and I would have you ever remember that you are being educated in an institution built by the hand of the Lord, and that you are not to live for yourselves." We should add that Miss Lyon continued to speak words like these, each succeeding year of her life, to those whom she was so happy as to call her pupils, and perhaps no one ever left her to be happy in living for herself.

None of those early pupils can ever forget the recitation rooms, where Miss Lyon made them delight in Whately's Logic and Butler's Analogy; and we can see her even now with Edwards' History of Redemption in her hand, and seem to feel that we are again seated with her in that first reading-room of the seminary, listening to the story of the wondrous plan for saving man. In her teachings, we found Christ on every page of the Old Testament. She led us on from that first promise to Adam, lying so low in his fall, through types and shadows pointing to the Messiah, till, with Isaiah, we stood on the mountain-top, and could see the Desire of all nations coming to his holy temple. We discovered then a fullness in Christ, not before understood, and we sang the hymn of our childhood with new delight: —

> "Holy Bible, book divine,
> Precious treasure" —

Those readings of Edwards were always between the morning and afternoon service of the Sabbath, and the attendance upon them was entirely voluntary. We are sure that all who learned of Christ through Edwards and Mary Lyon will thank God throughout eternity for those blessed seasons.

And they will thank him also for the Bible Lessons that followed on Monday morning. Miss Lyon always expected us to make ourselves familiar with every thing in the Bible in reference to the individuals or scenes brought before us. She was at home in all that God had said of them; and when she saw that we were also, she would make us recognize God's hand in every thing. And did we not fear him, as we went with her, over five hundred years, from the destruction of Jericho, to see Hiel come up from Bethel to build again the cursed city? And did we not tremble as we saw Abiram, his beloved first-born, fall in the beginning of the work? But still she led us on to see those gates of Jericho set up, and, amidst the joy and shouting as the top-stone was laid, we must go and stand by the grave of the youthful Segub, and remember that not a word that our God has spoken can be forgotten and not be fulfilled. Another Monday morning, she would lead us to feel that we should just as surely be left to worship a Baal, as did Ahab of old, if the child of Ethbaal must be our chosen friend.

But Miss Lyon's first year's pupils and all others must for ever remember those three mornings of the week, when she gathered all her family around her in the seminary hall, and unfolded religious truth. She always entered the hall carrying in her hand her cherished Bible, and a little village hymn-book, as she came from the secret place of the Most High to meet her pupils.

That "Good-morning, young ladies," which always fell from her lips before another word was spoken, made us know that there was certainly one heart on earth, that desired a *good morning* for us in its fullest sense. And it was good to be there. As the hymn was given out, we could see the glance of an eye that would know if we had all remembered our hymn-books. If some had forgotten, she would not then speak of it, but, perhaps, in the afternoon exercise, ask us all to read Deuteronomy, and note the words, "observe," "remember," "take heed," and see how God regards forgetfulness. There were those who realized in these words, for the first time, that forgetfulness may be a sin. And when we remembered how she had wished that her family, like the great family in heaven, might all praise God in singing, we always desired to join in the morning hymn. At another time she would say: "Secular music gives spirit and zest. We should thank God that he has so made us that we can enjoy it. It is wonderful kindness. Singing exerts a mighty moral influence, and, young ladies, I have no doubt that if you cultivate your musical powers here, you will sing and enjoy the song of Moses and the Lamb as those can not who have hidden their talent."

We realized that no other than her own Bible would answer her purpose, as we saw her follow the little path-finders placed in hers, and which enabled her to read in Exodus and then in Hebrews with so little delay that we hardly knew that she had passed from one to the other. She often said to us: "Young ladies, when I speak to you, I depend much more upon the inspiration of your countenances than on my preparation." That inspiration was fully given her in those exercises, and the preparation no less fully made when she was alone with her God. She felt the responsibility of no labor as much as this. What she wrote a friend a few weeks before her death expresses her uniform feeling: "I want to ask you to pray for me in a very special manner about one thing. It is for divine guidance and strength in giving religious instruction. Pray that I may have hid in my own heart all that I attempt to say. Pray that I may speak the words of truth, every jot and tittle, — that which God sees and knows to be truth. Pray that hearts may receive the truth in honesty, sincerity, and faith. Pray that in these seasons God may be magnified and glorified." At another time she said: "None but God knows how the responsibility of giving religious instruction to these candidates for eternity weighs on my heart. Sometimes, beforehand, my soul is weighed down with fear, trembling, and anxious solicitude, which finds no relief but in God. When I have finished, and God has given me some enlargement of heart, I am overwhelmed with gratitude, and with a view of my unworthiness for such a blessing. Then I can only pour out my heart in prayer that the Spirit may carry truth to the heart, though spoken in great weakness."

The giving of religious instruction included not only the morning exercises of three days in the week, but also the weekly meetings for Christians and the impenitent, all of which, she once said, "lie most heavily upon my heart. I often feel that I have used for you the last crumb that has fallen to me from the Master's table." It always seemed to us that she came before us with very choice portions from his table, and that one thus furnished might be willing to trust to the morrow for the manna of the morrow.

The house-keeping department of the new seminary had been considered a great objection to it by many. Miss Lyon labored to show her friends that she did not design a manual-labor school in any sense, nor a school where young ladies would be taught domestic duties; but rather one where they would practice what they had already learned from their mothers, — each pupil taking a daughter's part in the household duties, to relieve the necessity for domestics, and thus promote the happiness of the family. She told her first pupils, as she did all later ones, that they had not come to the seminary to learn domestic work, but to learn how to spend time profitably. Miss Lyon gave much time to this department, and was able to reduce every thing to beautiful order. But she was often heard to say: "This department is too complicated, and requires too much care to continue it, were it not for the great advantage it is to the family. If dollars and cents alone were concerned, we would drop it at once. Had I fully understood how complicated its working must be, perhaps I should never have undertaken it; but a kind Providence hid many of its difficulties from me, and I can see so much in it that is for the comfort of our household, and favorable to the young ladies individually, that I am willing to take all this extra care."

This care devolved mostly upon herself for years, till she saw the machinery all working smoothly, — till she had carefully adjusted wheel within wheel, and made every thing to move with the least possible friction.

Miss Lyon's own words will give us some of the advantages of this department as they lay in her own mind. She says: " All are to take part, not as a servile labor, for which they are to receive a small weekly remuneration, but as a gratuitous service to the institution of which they are members, designed for its improvement and elevation. We shall thus be relieved of dependence on private families in the neighborhood for board; and without this it will be difficult, if not impossible, to secure perpetual prosperity. We shall also be relieved from a depressing dependence on the will of hired domestics. We believe that the health and happiness of the young ladies will be promoted by this daily exercise, and their interest in domestic duties preserved. While no one receives reward for her services, no one will be able with her money to deprive herself of the privilege of sharing in the freedom, simplicity, and independence of her home. The institution *will not teach domestic duties.* This inestimable privilege will still be left to the mother. We can only seek to preserve the good habits already acquired, and to make a favorable impression with regard to the value of system, promptness, and fidelity in this branch of woman's duties.

"An obliging disposition is of special importance in forming a lovely, social, and domestic character. Young ladies at school, with all the conveniences and comforts which they *should* have, and with all the benefits of system which they should enjoy, can have but little opportunity for self-denial. This little should be used to the best advantage. To bring every such opportunity to bear on the character is a leading object in the arrangements of the family. The domestic work done by the young ladies, in the varied and mutual duties of the day, furnishes many little opportunities for the manifestation of a generous, obliging, and self-denying spirit, the influence of which we trust will be felt through life.

"It also helps to give a spirit of gratitude and a sense of obligation. Domestic life is little else but a continued scene of conferring and receiving favors. And how much of happiness depends on their being conferred with the manifest evidence of a willing heart, and on their being received with suitable tokens of gratitude! These two lovely traits go hand in hand, not often to be separated. The formation of a character that *can* be grateful is an object of special importance in a lady's education. Parents should seek to give their daughters privileges, and especially the means of an education, in a manner suited to lead them to realize that they are favors for which gratitude is due."

With such a view as has here been given of the importance of this department in Miss Lyon's estimation, it is no wonder that she could give heart and hand to carrying it forward. It was her greatest desire to have all find a happy home with her, — "one," as she often said, "something like the home above."

The pupils of that first year, most of whom were Christians, felt that this desire was realized. They saw "holiness" written not only on those walls, but upon every article within. They felt that they were not their own, and each moment was to them of more value than gold. We have seen that Miss Lyon's heart and hands were full. Mrs. Cowles says: "In all that year, she had never found an hour to spend in astonishment at her success and position." But when the duties of the year were all done, and she found herself on anniversary day in the crowded village church, surrounded by friends, the trustees of Mount Holyoke Seminary before her, her teachers at her side, and her pupils in the rear, the circumstances forced the view upon her, and wonder, gratitude, and praise filled her heart with a flood of emotions such as ordinary minds can not conceive. Her great soul was surcharged with pent-up joy. Smiles and tears strove for the mastery on her radiant face. She retired within herself, gave way to a joy with which no one could intermeddle, and for an hour resigned herself to the emotions of the occasion. None but her God knew through what she had passed to reach that hour, and he only knew how sincerely she then and there said, "This is not mine, but thine." With a Father's love, he directed all the exercises of that day to meet her feelings. The morning rose beautiful. The trustees and Dr. Hawes decided that the exercises — that is the address, and the giving of certificates to the senior class of three, — should be in the church. She had shrunk from so much publicity, but when they said to her, "We think it is best," she was satisfied. Dr. Hawes' address was all she could desire. Mr. Condit, the pastor of the church in South Hadley, and secretary of the Board of Trustees, presented the certificates and gave farewell words in "his own happy manner," just as he continued to give them for ten years to succeeding classes.

One, who has often been present on anniversary occasions at Mount Holyoke Seminary, has said: "Miss Lyon never appeared better than on such days. Kindness, gentleness, ease, and dignity of manner were always very marked. She was never disconcerted, never in a hurry, and always seemed to have time to see every one, and to give appropriate attention to all that was laid upon her. There was at such times scope for all her powers. They were brought into action, and, as I have seen her preside on such occasions, I have felt that I was permitted to behold the highest style of woman performing her duties in a manner which reflected great honor upon her sex."

Such was her appearance on that first anniversary day, while, with a full heart, she wrote "Immanuel" on each passing event.

CHAPTER IX.

Second, Third, and Fourth Years.

SECOND YEAR, 1838 — MARRIAGE OF MISS CALDWELL — REVIVAL OF THAT YEAR — THIRD YEAR, 1839 — THE REVIVAL — DEATH OF A PUPIL — FOURTH YEAR, 1840 — EPIDEMIC SICKNESS AMONG THE PUPILS — THE REVIVAL — FIRST MEETING WITH PUPILS.

THE second year of Mount Holyoke Seminary, one hundred were admitted, while, to about four hundred, Miss Lyon was obliged to say: "There is no more room." Miss Caldwell, the Associate Principal, left the institution at the close of the first year, and married Rev. J. P. Cowles. Miss Lyon felt the loss most deeply; but she gave her friend a farewell, just as she did others in later years, with tears and smiles, saying: "We should be happy to have you with us longer, but we will be thankful that you have been able to do so much for us; God bless you." Miss Lyon was often called upon to give up teachers to whom her heart clung with an elder sister's love, and whom she considered almost indispensable to the seminary; but, while she said, "Of all the changes that take place, the changing of fellow-laborers, of fellow-travelers through this pilgrimage is the most painful," it was never with a murmur, and the departing one felt as she had not done before, that she lived, and should ever live in Miss Lyon's love.

Miss Whitman, for many years associated with Miss Lyon, and at this time a pupil in the seminary, thus describes the blessing of that year: "The second year the number regarding themselves as unconverted was about thirty. During that year God manifested his acceptance of the consecrated institution, not by a visible cloud, but by a baptism of the Holy Ghost. The work was very rapid and advanced with great power. It occurred in connection with the fast for literary institutions. The whole school bowed beneath its influence. The breathings of the Spirit were felt in every heart. The lukewarm professor and the openly irreligious alike trembled for their personal safety. The light footstep, the hushed voice, and the solemn countenance indicated the thoughts of all hearts. Many a slumbering professor awoke to newness of life.

"During the three days succeeding the last Thursday in February, which had been sacredly observed by the teachers and scholars as a season of fasting and prayer, about one half of the impenitent indulged the hope of having passed from death unto life. Saturday of the same week was a day of recreation. In the afternoon nearly the whole school came together, filling to its utmost capacity the reading-room where the meeting was held. After continuous prayer for an hour, the meeting was appropriately closed by one of the teachers. No one rose to leave the room. The feeling pervaded the circle that prayer must be continued until every soul was converted. Another prayer was then offered, after which the same teacher proposed that all should retire to their rooms for half an hour, and then those who desired should meet again in the same place. At the end of the half hour the burdened souls came together to plead once more for their companions who were still out of Christ. But one that year remained destitute of the Christian hope. Many were the prayers offered for that halting one, and in after years it was found that praying breath had not been spent in vain. She has since died in peaceful hope of divine acceptance, referring its origin to that second year of Mt. Holyoke Seminary.

"Thus did the young seminary receive its baptism of the Spirit. Thus did God accept as his own the institution which had been privately and publicly consecrated to him by donors, the trustees, and most of all by her, who, standing at its head, was often heard earnestly pleading that not one of all who should enjoy its privileges down to the millennial day, should fail of eternal life." Miss Whitman has well added: "The effects of such a work were felt for several successive years."

Not only Miss Lyon, but many others, had at that time, as she expressed it, "a very deep sympathy with others as saved or lost." She added: "We are so constituted, that we can not in this world sustain a great depth of feeling continually; this is reserved for another world. But we should feel deeply at times. It has an influence upon our after lives." Perhaps this was never more true of any season than of the one just described. Its most thrilling scenes were hardly passed, when death entered the seminary for the first time; but it was to bear a child to her heavenly home, and to lead Miss Lyon to pray, more earnestly than ever before, that in all her efforts she might be preparing souls for heaven.

The third year opened as the preceding, with the house filled, and hundreds unable to gain admittance. The trustees, at Miss Lyon's earnest solicitation, were now beginning to plan for enlarging the building. While she was exceedingly anxious to have this done, she was no less anxious lest, becoming engrossed by it, she should lose a spiritual blessing. Her Father saw her desire that he should be honored, and led her very gently, till her entire school were indulging the Christian hope. Thirty expressed that hope for the first time. Miss Whitman says of that year: "The work was gradual and there was a continued interest from the first week of the school till its close. The presence of the Spirit was manifested from the first by attention to instruction, the tearful eye, and exhibition of tenderness of feeling, whenever the subject of personal religion was introduced."

One, who was then a pupil, thus describes the beginning of this work of grace: "It was our third Saturday evening in the seminary. The day had been one of recreation, and we had enjoyed just what Miss Lyon had always said she wished us to enjoy, 'lively, pleasurable, social intercourse.' As we gathered around the tables for our evening meal, there was one table where she saw unbecoming mirth; there was even frivolity, and most of those at that table were professing Christians. As we sat back for our evening devotions, Miss Lyon rose, and said in a manner that made us feel that it is a fearful thing for a Christian to grieve the Spirit of God: 'I have thought that perhaps some of God's dear children here do not know that his Spirit is striving with some souls in our family. There are those who long to find a Saviour before this Sabbath has passed. Would you not like to pray for them?' Not another word was spoken. Careless Christians felt that they were on holy ground, and more than one of the impenitent buried her face to weep, finding her half-formed purpose to seek the Lord strengthened. As we passed out, a stranger threw her arm around me, saying: 'You do not know me, but I thought perhaps you would pray for me, that I may find Christ this Sabbath-day.' I had been reproved by Miss Lyon's words, and now my God brought still another reproof. I sought my closet to weep, and to feel that, if a child of God, I must be ready always to pray and to labor for souls."

Many Christians left that room with similar feelings, and those few words of Miss Lyon seemed given to guide them all the year, and we know that they have led many to watch carefully all their lives, lest by any means they grieve the Spirit of God from an inquiring soul.

From the very commencement of this term, it was noticed that Miss Lyon often prayed that God would especially prepare for heaven any whom he was about to take to himself. There was an earnestness in these petitions that we can not describe. It sometimes seemed as if it must be that she saw heaven's gates opening to receive her dear pupils, and that thus she was moved to ask for them this abundant entrance into the world of light and love. A few weeks passed, and, as she had seemed to expect, the Saviour came to take one of his own to himself. The heart that had prayed so earnestly was now in tenderest sympathy with the departing one. She watched the progress of a slow fever for weeks, expecting that her pupil would recover; but saw, at length, that this sickness was unto death. The dying one feared no evil in going through the appointed valley, and it was Miss Lyon's blessed privilege to come and place a rod and a staff in her hand for the passage. It was the midnight hour of the Sabbath when the attendants first realized that Jesus had indeed come for their sister.

One who was present says: "Miss Lyon asked me to go for her at any hour when there should be a change that indicated Miss H.'s speedy departure. Wearied and worn as she was, I disliked to call her; but this hesitation was removed as I heard her say: 'When Jesus comes for one of my dear children, I want to go with her just as far as I can. I do not expect to pass over with our dear friend at this time, but may be the Lord will give me a word wherewith to comfort her, and may be, as I see heaven open, I shall get a new view of its blessedness, to give to those who remain.' As I awaked Miss Lyon from sleep, she said: 'Do you think the Saviour has really come for Adaline?' She was by her side in a few minutes to realize that it was even so. The dying one could not speak, but her eye kindled with a brightness hardly of earth when she saw her teacher approaching. Miss Lyon knelt at once by her side, and, taking her hand in hers, said, in the gentlest manner: 'Jesus has come for you, Adaline. Now you will not be afraid, — will you? He will carry you safely over. You have nothing to do but to look directly to him. You will suffer only a little while longer.' Then she prayed in words as simple as she had spoken. The dying one could not tell us that she was comforted, but we knew it, for her eye would rest one moment on Miss Lyon, and then, with a smile, it would be turned upward to see the Saviour to whom she had been pointed. More than twenty years have passed since that sad November night, during all of which I have thanked my God for the lesson I there learned, of speaking only of Jesus to those for whom he is waiting. In this case the groans and dying strife were continued long after the eye closed upon us, and when it seemed to us that the ear could no longer hear the name she had delighted to have whispered to her.

"It was not till sunset on Monday that there was the calm which death brings. There had been such intense sympathy with the sufferer that many of the family were unfitted for attention to their ordinary duties. Those who had heard the departing sighs, and realized the pain and not the bliss of dying, were sad, and longed to pillow their aching heads upon a mother's bosom. Miss Lyon saw how we felt, and with more than a mother's love she gathered us around her to point beyond. She told us what joy seemed to fill our sister's heart, as she was directed to Jesus, and added: 'Why should she not have rejoiced? To be sure there was suffering for a little season, but I felt that she saw Christ during all the time that the finishing process of taking down the tabernacle was going on. We, who stood by, could almost see him, and we too did groan earnestly, desiring to be clothed upon from heaven. My own heart was so filled with thoughts of the blessedness of the departing soul, that I could think of nothing else. That room where our dear Adaline left her body, to see Jesus as he is, is a very precious spot to me. I should love to go and stay there for a season, — yes, there where heaven was opened to receive one of our number. Jesus has honored it, for he came there, just as he said he would, to receive one of his dear children to himself. I did not say good-by to Adaline when I saw her eye closing in death, for I am confident that I shall see her again soon. What glories burst upon her view in that room! It can never be to us like other rooms, and who of you would like now to go in there, and abide with Christ the remainder of this year? We will all thank God that he did not call for one of you who had no Saviour to come for her, and to whom we must have said good-by, and that for ever. I could not then have sat here this morning to speak of the state of such an one. My whole soul would have shrunk from it. Now I should like to talk to you all day of the state of those who have laid aside their earthly tabernacles and have gone to be with their Lord.'

"As we heard Miss Lyon speak of our dear friend in heaven, and of the 'blessed room' where she took the hand of Jesus, so much gentler than that even of father, mother, brother, or sister, we were comforted. We passed up from the seminary hall to the room, glad to make it ours, and it became the place of a daily prayer-meeting during all that year."

It was a special comfort to Miss Lyon, at the close of this school year, that she could look upon all her family as Christ's. She felt that much had been attained in thoroughness, and she was looking forward to another year with fond hopes of rich spiritual and temporal blessing. But at this point, to use her own words: "God saw that great trials must be set over against great prosperity." The anniversary season of 1840 had just passed, and the pupils were mostly in their homes, when one after another fell sick of typhus fever, till forty cases were heard of, and nine were called to their heavenly home. Miss Lyon had prayed much that all who were to go might be prepared for the change, and it was not surprising that dying grace was wonderfully given to dying ones. "O death, where is thy sting? O grave, where is thy victory?" was the song of triumph that was heard from each, as she turned away from earth to realize that God giveth the victory through our Lord Jesus Christ.

During the year now closed it had been customary

for Christians in the seminary to meet together in small circles for prayer at sunset on Sabbath evening. Those were very precious seasons, where hearts were made one in Jesus; and, as they met on the last Sabbath evening of the year, there was given on the part of all the members of our circle, a pledge of remembrance at the same hour, when they should be separated. Three weeks passed, and that Sabbath houı found most of the little circle on beds of sickness, but all remembered that it was the hour of prayer. One, on whom heaven was opening, prayed for the others, and then said: "Mother, they will pray for me now. They will not know that I am dying, but I am so happy to think they will pray for me." Another, as she asked the hour, said: "I should be glad to go while they are praying for me;" while a third said to weeping friends around her: "There will come peace, for they are praying God to bless me." One was released from earth at that hour of prayer, and others gathered strength to soon follow, while the Lord said to some longing to depart: "Ye can not come to me, now, but grace shall be given you to meet the ills of life, as you go back from this view of your final rest."

There was fullness of joy in Christ bestowed upon all who then died; and to those who came back to earth there was given an experience of his preciousness and of trust in him that they had not known before.

But, while the departing ones rejoiced, all the "waves and billows" seemed to be rolling over Miss Lyon. In writing a friend soon after, she says: "The hand of God has been laid heavily upon me. I have been led through deep waters; but they have not overflowed me. His good hand has been ever my support. None but my heavenly Father knows how great a trial this has been to my heart. While others have been inquiring about the natural cause, I have felt that we, who were most nearly connected, ought particularly to inquire about the moral cause, and to seek to know what the Lord would have us learn from his dealings with us." Miss Lyon was always as ready to learn as a child; and now she sought very carefully to know if her Father would have her change any thing in the arrangements for her great family. After much prayer and consultation with friends, some changes were made. And while the great plans went on as usual, she said: "If our feelings are grieved by what is reported of us, let us remember the example of our Saviour. He was silent. He opened not his mouth. Let God, in his own way and in his own time, vindicate his own acts. Let us commit ourselves to the care of a covenant-keeping God, who doeth all things well."

When the school assembled on the last day of September, 1840, hardly half of those expected had re-urned. Several had gone to be with God, and others were detained by sickness. Yet the house was filled, for there were many ready to take the places of those who had failed. Miss Lyon said of her trial: "The dealings of Providence have been such toward me as to lead me to think most tenderly of *all* my friends." And her reception of her pupils was now peculiarly tender. She was borne down with deep sorrow; but she met them cheerfully, and gave herself most unreservedly to labor, till her failing strength took her from them. We have before us the note-book of a pupil who entered the seminary on that day, a stranger, which shows how the new scholars were impressed with her appearance. The note-book says: "The young ladies, eighty in number, met in the seminary hall at nine o'clock. Miss Lyon read a Psalm, and led in a prayer, which was very comprehensive and affecting. The burden of her petition was that, if any one present had never given herself to Christ, she might now be led to do so, even before she entered upon her studies; that the blessings of life and health might crown the year, if consistent with our heavenly Father's will; but if any were to be removed by death, that they might here ripen for heaven."

It pleased the Lord to grant life and health this year, and another blessed outpouring of the Spirit. There was a hopeful conversion the very first week of the year; and the work went on, till, of the thirty who entered the school, not Christians, Miss Lyon could write: "All but four now express some hope that they love Christ."

In the midst of her sore trial, her thoughts turned more to the goodness of God than to any other theme; and she gave this subject for the Bible lesson of the first Sabbath of the term. A pupil, who, from her first meeting Miss Lyon, seemed to be in full sympathy with her, wrote of that day: "The sun rose in brightness, as if God, in his goodness, had chosen that the first pleasant day of our residence here should be the Sabbath, that our associations with the day should be pleasant." The Bible lesson had been given out on Saturday; and as Miss Lyon alluded to it at the breakfast-table the next morning, when her pupils were seated for devotions, she said: "Now we hope to spend forty Sabbaths together; and will not those who fear the Lord speak often one to another? Then will he write for us a book of precious remembrance; for he has said he will do it. We expect to pray together here forty Sabbath mornings. Then we shall separate, never all to meet again in this world; and we have some dear ones, who have no hope of meeting us beyond this life. May not such a hope be given to some of them this first Sabbath morning?" This bringing home of the subject of being a Christian on that morning, when so many were strangers, and when her own heart was so tender, deeply affected many. They could not easily lose the impression; and, when, in the afternoon, they came together, and she pointed them to the heaven where nine pupils had just entered, most of whom she had expected would sit there on that Sabbath, their hearts were more deeply moved. She spoke of heaven as no strange place. She said: "We can know much of heaven. If we have ever had feelings which we believe to be in unison with our heavenly Father's will, we then know something of the feelings enjoyed there."

There was something in Miss Lyon's first meeting with her pupils, that can not be described. We forgot the teacher, for we seemed only to see the mother, the friend, the Christian friend, one in whom our hearts could trust. Her interest in our parents and friends gave us a confidence in her, and then that cheerful countenance seemed to tell of a heart that could embrace us all. On the note-book of one pupil we find this record of remarks on the first morning of the school year, and many can recall words kindred to these: "There is always a peculiar interest in meeting our dear family at the commencement of the school year. We remember those dear familiar faces with us last year, which we shall see here no more. We thank our God for the precious privilege, which was ours, of laboring for those daughters. We follow them with our love, we will remember them around this family altar. We welcome old friends returning home with smiling countenances, and we also welcome these strangers. They will not long be strangers. Some of you are the daughters of those I tenderly love, and we are ready to give our love and sympathy to you all. My heart goes out very tenderly this morning to those parents who have intrusted you to my care. Those fathers and mothers have no choicer treasures than these precious daughters. We are ready to labor for you in love and fidelity, and may you all be faithful to us. And oh, what inexpressible tenderness in the thought, that you may all be preparing for heaven here!"

Another note-book records another year. "As Miss Lyon met us in the hall this first morning, she said: I shall not read a chapter from the Bible, but only a single verse, 'In every thing, by prayer and supplication with thanksgiving, let your request be made known unto God.' I could think of no other text as my thoughts turned to you. This is what I want you all to do every day this year. Carry every thing to God. There is nothing too small for his notice. When he says *every thing*, he means just what he says. Those who are Christians can do it, and those who are not may begin to do it to-day. Do not be afraid to do it because you know you are not a Christian. Does the heart of one such go out tenderly this morning to the friends she has left? Does any one feel anxious in reference to her examinations? Carry all to your heavenly Father. You may thus get an acquaintance with him that will make you long to say with a whole heart, *my* Father."

CHAPTER X.

Second, Third, and Fourth Years, Continued.

INFLUENCE OF TRIALS ON MISS LYON — SPECIMENS OF MORNING RELIGIOUS EXERCISES — DEATH OF HER MOTHER — HER SYMPATHY WITH THE BEREAVED — SPECIMENS OF AFTERNOON RELIGIOUS EXERCISES — HAD THE CONFIDENCE OF HER PUPILS — ANNIVERSARY ADDRESS BY PROF. EDWARDS.

THE trials of the autumn of 1840, made Miss Lyon, if possible, love the seminary more than ever before. She felt that she had been sorely chastised, but she wanted to know the lesson her Father would teach her, and she desired her pupils to learn the same. At the first meeting for Christians, she dwelt with peculiar interest upon their obligations to the benevolent founders of the institution. She had previously said: "On entering the seminary, young ladies can scarcely avoid feeling that they are sharing the fruits of benevolent efforts, and that they are enjoying privileges which they can not purchase; that they owe a debt of gratitude to the founders which gold and silver can never cancel, and which can be met only by a useful Christian life." She pressed this home more earnestly than ever, during this year, and especially at this meeting. After presenting other motives for faithfulness, she added: "This institution has been blessed of God, because it is his. It has been given to him; let us have no part in taking it back. And now there are those here who have come to this place with the hope of finding the Saviour. Shall we help them to do it?" There were Christian pupils this year, who labored diligently for souls, and who cared most faithfully for the young Christians as they were brought into the fold. We can understand Miss Lyon's confidence in them, as we find her saying to them, May 19th: "It is a solemn thought that all that most of us do for the four still impenitent in our family will be done in a few short weeks." Specimens of the morning exercises of this year are given in the Appendix.

We have brief notes, also, of some others of these morning exercises. At one time we find her taking the first epistle of Peter, and commenting upon a few verses each morning, while she asks her pupils to study it with her in their rooms. Fearing that Christians were not prepared to meet the Lord, she takes, on another morning, a part of the message to the seven churches, and leads them on to feel that they can not serve God and Mammon.

Early in the year, we find her explaining to Christians the office-work of the Spirit; his ordinary and extraordinary influences. And a little later, reading to the whole school passages on grieving that Spirit, and pointing out many ways in which it might be done, saying: "You may grieve the Spirit from your own heart and from other hearts. It may be done by thinking, doing, or speaking of unsuitable things at unsuitable times. It is a solemn thought, that a word or look may so influence another's mind, as to lead her to grieve away the Spirit. While God's essential presence is ever with us, he may be tempted to withdraw from us his blessing. It is easy so to grieve him that he shall leave us; and oh, how much more easily is he invited to stay with us, and to bless us!"

Prayer was dwelt upon, and it was shown that watchfulness and prayer, if sincere, can not be separated. They will walk hand in hand. The wrestling Jacob was one morning brought before the school, and they were led to feel that they need not let go of the Eternal One, even when he lays them so low that they can no more wrestle; and that the Christian often prevails when, God having touched him, he must lie passive in his hands.

Dec. 21, 1840, was observed as a day of fasting and prayer in the school, the pupils generally desiring it. It was not customary to appoint days of this kind so early in the year, but a special blessing followed this. A pupil made the following entry in her note-book on that day: "Miss Lyon's countenance was cheerful, and her instructions such as we needed. Her faith and hope seemed strong, yet humble. She recommended us to read portions of the Psalms and Prophets, the sixteenth and twenty-third chapters of Leviticus, and desired us to pray for them who had neglected to decide to profess Christ, and that others might be guided in their decisions; for those who are not sincere in their professions of interest; and for those just rejoicing in hope, that they might never go back. When she met us, in the afternoon, she spoke of the different classes of professing Christians; the backsliding, inconsistent, doubting, easily-tempted, deceived, and the active Christian. Her words were solemn and cheering."

Four days later, we find the following in the same note-book: "Miss Lyon read passages showing the plan of the divine government, — that this world was intended as a place of education for heaven, and where it is not so used, it has been perverted. It was designed that we should always exercise diligence and watchfulness. We are not to expect respite from labor, for if we can accomplish some things with facility, more will be given us to do. Our first great blessing is that we may be saved; the second, that we may labor for Christ."

Another morning, we find her dwelling upon a *uni-*

form, serious, Christian deportment. She said: "It can be obtained only by having the heart deeply impressed with eternal things," adding, "a want of uniformity, in this respect, is a great hindrance to Christian usefulness." The next day her subject was the propriety and importance of Christian rebuke, from the most delicate incidental question to open reproof. She said: "Never excuse yourselves because the person in fault has been told, or because she knew, her duty. The addition of your kind caution or reproof may be the means of saving her." This was the talk of the morning, while, in the evening meeting for Christians, she dwelt with great animation on the joys of heaven. A few days later, we find her speaking upon slander. One who knew Miss Lyon well, has said: "When this was her subject, we always felt that she not only told us what we ought to do, but what she was actually doing. For years I was intimately associated with her, but I never once heard from her lips an expression, in regard to another, that involved unkind feeling. There were no hard sayings of those not present. She never spoke lightly of a pupil."

There was perhaps no morning exercise of this year more impressive than that of Dec. 3, when Miss Lyon entered the school, as was her custom, with her great Bible on her arm. She had been absent for several days, watching by her dying mother, and as she looked around upon her pupils, and gave them her good-morning, there was an irresistible drawing of hearts toward her. She read 1 Thess. iv. 13, and one there present says: "She spoke to us affectionately of her dear mother, who, as she trusted, had been prepared many years to be called home. And now that the last object was removed which had shared her solicitude for her pupils, she desired to be more faithful to us, so that if at last all should not stand together on God's right hand, it might not be because she had been unfaithful." She gives expression to her deep feeling in a letter to Miss Grant. "I have now no mother or sister, whom I can go and see, and *alone* I followed my dear mother to the grave. Her prayers, which I have had daily for so many years, I shall have no more. She, to whose comfort I have been expecting the pleasant privilege of administering for years to come, as almost the only child left her, will need nothing more. I feel my family loneliness, but with it eternity seems very near, with all its precious privileges purchased by the blood of our glorious Saviour."

While Miss Lyon's thoughts and feelings turned so fully to eternity, she was still in time, and she suffered much in her health under these repeated strokes. During the winter following her mother's death, she says, she was "obliged to give over many portions of her work to others, and some weeks nearly all;" but adds: "I have felt that I have nothing to say, and scarcely any thing to ask but that God may be glorified." She was usually engrossed with labor, and said so little of personal matters, that few realized the strength of her attachment to her friends. Probably there was never a mother that received purer, stronger, and more lasting love than did the mother of Mary Lyon. She had honored and trusted that mother, sought her counsels and valued her prayers, and when she realized her departure, she says: "I felt a loneliness of which I had no previous conception." What Dr. Hitchcock says of Miss Lyon in another relation, we say in this: "How happy a mother must have been to receive such love from such a heart!" Her own strong feelings led her to understand those of others, and many can fully sympathize with the language of a pupil who says: "When that deep sorrow rolled over me, I was allowed to pillow my head on Miss Lyon's bosom. She drew me so near to her that I could feel the beatings of her own heart. One friend said to me, do this, and another said, do that; but Miss Lyon said: 'Rest here, my child, and we will ask God to take care of the whole matter.' And I did rest close by that heart of love, which seemed to understand my every feeling, and thankful to know that there were lips which could open only in gentleness when the soul was torn with grief."

The following extract from a letter, written soon after her mother's death, lays that heart open before us. The pupil to whom it is addressed was one who had suffered from the severe sickness of the previous autumn in person, and in the removal of a loved father and sister. Miss Lyon says: "Can you not come and stay with me a few days? I am not able to go out of my room much, and it would be a great comfort to me to have you with me. Dear one! I have felt for you most tenderly in your trials. They have been mine, and my feelings have been such that in my present state of health I have hardly dared to trust myself to write you. I want to talk with you of your loss, of our nine dear pupils who have gone to be with Christ, of my mother and sister, and of your own plans for the future. Do not try to do much. Rest, and rest here with me, if you can leave your mother. Arms of love wait to receive you."

When Miss Lyon met that pupil, some months later she felt that there were none other than arms of love thrown around her, and she says: "I can never forget how fast those tear-drops fell, as she silently laid her head upon my shoulder for a few brief moments, and then broke the silence by saying: 'How I do thank God, that he could spare you to come back to life! I know you would have been glad to go at once to heaven, but will you not also be happy in laboring a little longer for Christ?' There was to me a new view of the preciousness of laboring for Christ, as I looked upon that countenance where smiles and tears so met. I felt that only a heavenly hand should wipe away those tears. As I was with her for several days, she told me of her feelings as wave after wave of sorrow rolled over her during the autumn. She once said: 'When my pupils were dying one after another, I was afraid to take up a paper lest I should see some new name added to the deceased, and not have strength to meet it. I was afraid to ask a question, or even listen to conversation, lest I should not find myself prepared for what I might hear. There were days in which I could not attempt any thing except to ask God to hold me by his own hand. I had no heart to ask for any thing except to have my trust in God secured to me." After dwelling on this view for a time she added: 'But these events helped to prepare me for other trials that were soon to follow, in the taking from me of my mother and sister. And then to think of all those dear pupils in heaven. Oh, how good God was to make all his before he took any away! Heaven seems nearer to me than ever before, and labor on earth sweeter. A gentler and a safer hand than mine leads those who are gone. How comforting!'"

Miss Lyon said, near the close of life: "If trials

and perplexities come, then we may look for some comforting, consoling providence. We may always expect enough of trial and difficulty to make us love to sing, —

> 'Is this, dear Lord, that thorny road
> That leads us to the mount of God?"

and enough of consolation and support and blessing to make us feel that Christ's yoke is easy and his burden light." While the trials of this year were severe, the blessings were great.

During the summer of 1841, Miss Lyon left her school and took a journey with her kind friends, Dea. and Mrs. Safford. She returned with renewed health and every thing around comforted her. The new building was so far advanced that she could receive a larger number of pupils the coming year. There was almost perfect health in the school, and there had been a rich blessing of the Spirit, such an one that Miss Lyon herself said: "It seems to me that I never had a school in which there was more of the spirit of heaven." She was obliged to relinquish much of her teaching in the class-room this year, but, so far as able, she gave the religious instruction, and also often met the school in a general exercise in the afternoon. At such times all were assembled in the seminary hall and the talks were of a miscellaneous, but strictly practical, character. They were valued at the time, but far more in after life when circumstances led to applying them. One, who long since left the seminary, has said: "There is not a day of my life in which I do not recall those afternoon exercises of Miss Lyon. My increasing experience of life increases my admiration, both of her ability to select topics on which to counsel us, and her power to make so permanent an impression on our minds. She certainly understood the will of the Lord as fully as Paul, and in secular no less than in spiritual matters." We give notes of a few of the afternoon exercises of that year, just as they were written at the time by pupils.*

These afternoon exercises were entered into with so much interest, that, for the time, one would suppose that Miss Lyon's heart was so fully in them that there could be no thought for the evening meeting that was to follow. But she could turn from one to the other with perfect ease because with her all was done for God.

We have seen her in the afternoon cause the greatest merriment as she drew the picture of a family wanting in promptness (she would make certain courses of conduct appear ridiculous, but never ridiculed persons), and, when the evening came, there would be a holy, delightful calm as we gathered around her to have her point us to Christ, our Mediator, standing at the right hand of the Father, and making this a

* See Appendix, p. 235.

reason why we should live holy lives. "Yet," she added, "you will not all manifest your Christian character in the same way; you are variously constituted. Perhaps some of you are inclined to be very silent. Now we wish you to correct this as far as it is an evil. But being a Christian will not make such a person talk all the time; neither should it cause a very lively person to be silent. Honor God with the constitution he has given you, keeping your peculiar temperaments and tendencies in perfect control. It is not wise for a Peter to try to be a John, but rather to be the best Peter possible, and John to be the best John possible, rather than seek to be a Paul. Then she would address young Christians with great tenderness, beseeching them not to go back to the trifles and vanities of this world, and encouraging them to go forward, because Christ loves to fulfill his precious promises to individuals; and she would add: "And why, dear young friends, should you not be the individuals to know the fullness of these promises?"

Miss Lyon sympathized so fully with the feelings of her pupils that they seldom made plans for doing any thing, not even the giving of a present, without her approbation. One says on this point: "We were sure, if it was best to do it, she would favor it; but, if she saw reasons for not pursuing our plan, we could cheerfully relinquish it." She often made such remarks as the following to her pupils: "I do not think the giving of presents should be greatly encouraged, and still it is at times highly proper. We sometimes receive favors, and there are public services rendered which money can not repay, and in some gift we can show the friend who has conferred them that they are held in grateful remembrance. If the gift can be the work of our hands, something which costs time rather than money, it will only be the more acceptable. Making presents sometimes cultivates a spirit of selfishness, because gifts are expected in return. Those who are most ready to give splendid presents are not, usually, the most ready to give to benevolent objects, and thus a high standard of benevolence is not cultivated."

After listening to such sentiments as these, we are not surprised to find the following entries in the note-book from which we have already drawn: —

Nov. 16, 1840. "Miss — and I went to Miss Lyon's room to propose a plan for giving Mr. Hyde (the steward) a present. She favored it, expressing the hope that it would not diminish our missionary contribution. It is remarkable how she takes every thing into view."

Nov. 22. "Miss Lyon sent for four of us to talk with us about the present. How she remembers every thing! Each young lady gave six and a quarter cents, and we presented Mr. Hyde sixteen volumes of the Evangelical Family Library."

There was a peculiar satisfaction to the pupils, generally, in having Miss Lyon know all that was going forward, and this is but one of a thousand cases where her counsel and approbation were sought. We may, perhaps, here give the testimony of another to Miss Lyon's comforting words: "There was a sick one in our family, for whom Miss Lyon wished me to care Finding that one of my recitations was Ecclesiastical History, and that I had before studied it, she told me, if I would take care of the suffering one, I should be excused from the review of the book at the close of the year, as well as from a public examination. But when the time came, I heard my name read, and was called to duty. I spoke to the teacher of the class about being excused from it by Miss Lyon; but she thought there was a mistake, and I must recite. I spoke to her the second time with a full heart, when she said: 'I think you are mistaken, but we will go to Miss Lyon.' In a moment we were by Miss Lyon's side, and her cheerful 'What is it, Miss ——?' led me to begin to say: 'Am I mistaken, Miss Lyon, in thinking that you said I might be excused from the review?' Here she took the words from my lips: 'I know, dear, your History. Why, no, dear, you are not mistaken. Was your name read?' Her kindness brought tears, and the tears brought her hand to wipe them away, saying: 'Certainly you are excused, and do you not wish to be excused from something else? I have not forgotten what you did for the sick one.' I could not answer; and seeing this, she said with a smile: 'Did you know that Deacon and Mrs. Porter are expected this afternoon? Would you not like to come and help me arrange the room for them?' Oh, how thankful I was for the kindness and for the wisdom that turned my heart-throbbings into another channel, by giving me something to do!"

But the kindness manifested this year was only a repetition of the kindness of other years, and her interest in her pupils at home, as expressed in the following paragraph, only the interest of every year. "Miss Lyon spoke of the ways of doing good, after we return home, by creating and sustaining an interest in female prayer-meetings, by manifesting an abiding interest in the Sabbath school, either as teacher or scholar, by religious conversation, by seeking out and benefiting the poor, by instructing children in religious and other subjects, and by our deportment at home. Our friends will expect much when we return; our Saviour will expect much. We may do much to elevate the standard of piety in those around us."

The year of blessings following the sore trials of the autumn of 1840 was closed by the anniversary address given by Prof. B. B. Edwards, of Andover. When Dr. Anderson had been invited two years before to give the anniversary address, many friends had sought to dissuade him from bestowing his influence on such an enterprise; but Prof. Edwards had advised him to do it, and now he himself stood in the same place, to give one of the choicest productions of his gifted mind and pen. It was a fitting close for the school year.

CHAPTER XI.

Fifth and Sixth Years.

FIFTH YEAR, 1841 — ENLARGEMENT OF THE SEMINARY BUILDING — DAILY PRAYER-MEETINGS BEGUN — SIXTH YEAR, 1842 — ASSISTANT TEACHERS — WEEKLY MEETINGS OF THE TEACHERS — TEACHERS' PRAYER-MEETING.

IN October, 1841, the seminary was again thronged. The new building was not ready for occupancy till December, but Miss Lyon told us we could certainly be very happy in close quarters with the prospect of such ample provision the remainder of the year. The whole was anew given to the Lord. The dews of the Spirit began to descend very early, and the cloud seemed hardly to be lifted during the whole year; yet at its close more were left out of Christ than the preceding year. This year was marked as one of great growth in Christian character. Many who had been prevented from returning the previous year by the sickness of the autumn of 1840, were now present, and they sat as learners, with new interest, at the feet of her who had had fresh experience of heavenly guidance during their absence.

It was during this year that little daily prayer-meetings were commenced. The form of these meetings has been somewhat changed since that time, but they have been constantly continued. When instituted, they were called "neighborhood meetings." Suitable rooms were chosen in different parts of the house, and all were invited to attend. Teachers were never present on these occasions, — the meetings being conducted by the pupils themselves. In some of these circles as many different individuals had charge as there were days in the week. Monday was given to Foreign Missions, and she who had the care of the meeting said a few words suggesting particular subjects under this head. Then followed voluntary prayers, till the time had expired. Tuesday was given in the same way to Home Missions. Wednesday, to prayer for the Bible and Tract Societies. Thursday, to home churches and friends. Friday, to our own and other seminaries, while on Saturday we pleaded for Abraham's seed, and prayed, " Thy kingdom come in *all* the world." There was something in thus praying together that united Christian hearts very closely, and we expected to hear from week to week of blessings on those for whom we had sought to the Lord. There was always opportunity for any one at the meeting to present special requests for prayer; and, as many of those not Christians attended, there sometimes came a message like this: "While you pray for the perishing heathen, pray for a perishing sister in your own family." Though Miss Lyon never attended these meetings, yet her heart was in them, and, as she saw the crowds pass out, she would say: "Let me decrease, if I may only see these increase."

The autumn of 1842 opened with the enlarged seminary filled to overflowing, and, desirous of doing all that could be done for the school, Miss Lyon made the number of teachers larger than before. Six new ones were added to the list, while Misses Moore and Whitman, made associate principals, bore the seminary upon their hearts with hardly less interest than Miss Lyon herself. We love to remember what Miss Lyon did and how God honored her in that work; but her hands were stayed up by two as faithful servants as were given Moses in the hour of conflict. Misses Moore and Whitman entered fully into all Miss Lyon's plans, and most faithfully did they carry out what she devised. The younger teachers looked upon the three as of one mind, and one of those teachers has said: "With the love that I bore to Miss Lyon, I could love any one who helped her faithfully, and met her every desire." We can hardly see that Misses Moore and Whitman were less esssential to the prosperity of the infant seminary than Miss Lyon herself; and her words in reference to the trustees apply to them:

"They were raised up just when needed, and w e continually receiving fresh anointings from the Lord for their service."

Mrs. Cowles has described Miss Lyon's teachers as no one could who had not been one of them: "They regarded her with mingled love, confidence, and veneration, entered enthusiastically into her views, and saw in her the servant of the Lord raised up for the very work that she was doing. In selecting her assistants, Miss Lyon's first question was not, Are you of one religious denomination or another? but, Are you like the Lord Jesus Christ, willing to make yourselves poor, that others through your poverty may be rich?" And Mrs. C. says that when they accepted an invitation from Miss Lyon to be with her, it was with "a desire to do good" combined "with the pleasure of unfolding minds of a higher order, delight in communing with congenial spirits, the identification of the seminary with themselves, and the luxury of living in what seemed to them a miniature paradise, and of anticipating the millennial glory."

Their pupils were from an intelligent class, the course of study from year to year was extended, and Mrs. C. has justly said of those teachers: "A solemn sense of accountability to God for the right use of their time and faculties, secured a higher standard of study and recitation among scholars than any motives drawn from the world of time and sense could have done. The fear of the Lord is indeed wisdom and instruction."

Miss Lyon was accustomed to refer to her teachers before the school in a manner that led the young ladies to see how much she esteemed them, and at the same time to realize that she expected they would give themselves entirely to their work. We copy the following from a note-book, bearing date October, 1842: "Such is the value of immortal beings, that all who have the care of youth ought to make every sacrifice for their good, and, if need be, perhaps lay down their lives. With this motive in view, the teachers in this school endeavor to make it the best possible in their power. I believe that the love and respect of the young during the whole progress of their education are best secured by those teachers who pursue plans best adapted to their improvement. Teachers may be strict without harshness, and, having decided upon what is best, they should seek to carry it out in the most kind and acceptable manner."

Another note-book of a later year says: "Miss Lyon said to us, — 'I feel that these teachers are placed here by the special providence of God, and therefore they may expect, in seeking to him, to know his will. We shall wish to do what is right, kind, and benevolent. We hope and expect that you will be glad to meet our requirements. I think that proper parental government is a beautiful illustration of the principles and spirit of the divine government, and I think that school government should be made the same. It is, indeed, sometimes more like the divine government than the parental, because the latter is more liable to be vitiated by parental fondness.'" She never feared to speak to her school of what a teacher's qualifications should be. She once said, when both teachers and pupils were present: "If you would be good teachers, you must seek to have your minds meet other minds. You must be able to take charge of any part of a child's education; try to lead in the path of universal wisdom."

Weekly meetings of the teachers were held for mutual consultation and prayer. Miss Lyon met her assistants as an elder sister, and there was no clashing of opinions among them. One of those teachers, under date of Oct. 23, 1846, thus writes: "This is our evening for teachers' business meeting. We had a very pleasant time. After the business was finished, Miss Lyon went down and had a quantity of peaches brought up; then she said: 'I wish you all to consider yourselves as visitors and to enjoy yourselves as much as possible. I can not talk" (she was suffering from a severe cold), "but I can see your smiling faces and enjoy it all, though I can not hear very well.'" Under another date, the same writer says: "At the close of the teachers' meeting, Miss Lyon said: 'We have a great work to do. Let us be faithful to these dear children. How many parents' hearts are beating with anxious hopes for our dear charge! I like to think what a number of Christian parents are connected with our school. It is a privilege to spend and be spent for their children; above all, let us seek their spiritual welfare. Let us keep in mind that our great work is to seek the salvation of souls.' At another meeting, Miss Lyon said: 'Now I would like to know if any of you has too much to do. Tell me frankly if it is so. There may have been some oversight, that has given some one of you more than her share of labor. Do not be afraid to speak of it; if you tell me, it will only help me to give you more when you can bear it. I know you all esteem it a privilege to do what you can.'

"At the close of another business meeting, these words fell from her lips: 'I think we should be very careful to observe the general regulations of our family; try to be systematic. I have suffered all my life from the want of regular habits. I wish you to accustom yourselves to be thoroughly systematic in the division of your time and duties. I know you have many interruptions, and many little things to look after; but so it must be with ladies. I really think it requires more discipline of mind and more grace to meet a lady's duties than a gentleman's. He has little of minutiæ to attend to. He can rise in the morning and go to his business without hindrance; but it is not so with a lady, and I would not have it otherwise.'"

Near the time of a vacation, and when Miss Lyon was not able to labor herself, we find the following in a letter: "Miss Lyon is rather better. We met in her room as usual for business on Friday evening. She said, 'she knew, that the few days before we should separate would be days of great importance. She hoped we should be faithful. She felt that she was herself almost a cumberer of the ground, but she did sympathize with us in our many labors.'" Miss Lyon's teachers always felt that she sympathized with them. It was always easy to work with her. They were assured that they really helped her, and no mother's heart was perhaps ever more gratified for an unexpected favor, or relief when weary and worn, than Miss Lyon. One who often guarded her door carefully that she might sink into unconsciousness and thus renew her prostrated energies, says: "Miss Lyon almost made me think that I had done an angel's work, as she came out of her room, so bright, and said: 'Oh, I am so thankful to you for this rest! You have really given me strength for many days of labor.'"

Besides the business meetings, Miss Lyon held a

prayer-meeting with her teachers, when she encouraged them in their labors for souls. They went out of those meetings with new strength, and with the conviction that every soul for whom they cared was borne by Miss Lyon to the Lord Jesus. We add extracts from letters, which show the spirit of these prayer-meetings. The first was written soon after the close of a vacation. "We had our teachers' prayer-meeting in Miss W.'s room. Each teacher's section was remembered, — those who had become Christians, and those still interested, but not Christians. Miss Lyon spoke of the importance of being faithful, especially in our closets, and said: 'We shall doubtless be tried. It must be precept upon precept, and prayer upon prayer.' She closed by saying: 'All may be dark to us, but, like Noah's dove, we may find a rare, a sweet resting-place with our God. He *can not* fail us.'"

The same writer says, under a later date in that year: "In our teachers' prayer-meeting, Miss Lyon requested us to mention any, not Christians, whom we would like to have prayed for. Two were mentioned; and then we knelt down and prayed for them; and then two more, and so on, till twelve were mentioned." A week later, the same says: "As at the last meeting, we remembered individuals in our prayers. One for whom we then prayed is now indulging hope. Miss

Lyon said: 'Let us pray, expecting an answer.'" Of the last teachers' prayer-meeting of that term, we find the following: "What shall we pray for while we are separated? Let us remember all the family; pray for all the Christians, that they may be more and more consecrated to God; that they may be kept from temptation. Let us pray for those with whom the Holy Spirit is still striving." She then proposed that the names of all those without hope should be mentioned. They were all mentioned, and we prayed for them. Miss Lyon then remarked: "We never had a year like this before, when the Holy Spirit tarried so long with us by his special influences."

In the middle of the last term of that year we find Miss Lyon saying, in one of those teachers' meetings: "Let us make most faithful effort, during these last few weeks, that no one soul among us be neglected." At another meeting still, Miss Lyon proposed that subjects of prayer be mentioned for the ensuing week; and requested the teachers to pray that the young ladies might succeed in their studies and in doing right; and that the teachers might have the privilege and the wisdom to help them to do right.

In the records of those teachers' prayer-meetings we also find how Miss Lyon remembered those who had gone out from her. The following notes are from the journal of Mrs. Mills, whose husband has been connected for some years with Oahu College, at the Sandwich Islands.

"April 5. At our teachers' prayer-meeting this evening, after singing, Miss Lyon said: 'We will now unite in two prayers for those who once met with us in this capacity, and who are now on missionary ground or on their way thither.'

"June 4. Miss Lyon again asked us to remember all who had ever taught in the seminary, and especially those who were now missionaries, and proposed that we should have stated times of praying for them.

"June 18. At teachers' meeting, Miss Lyon spoke with interest of a little note from Mrs. B. (a missionary), and then proposed that the names be mentioned of all those who had once been here, but who were now missionaries either at home or abroad. So each of us mentioned one or more, till the names of all were repeated. We then united in two prayers for them, Miss Lyon leading in one. She said: 'Let us be faithful, and we shall meet these friends in heaven.'"

Eternity alone can tell how much of blessing was bestowed upon those teachers and pupils laboring in our own and other lands, in answer to the prayers offered for them by their friends in the seminary. Those absent ones have often said, as blessings descended upon them: "Some one is praying the prayer of faith for me." And why should not their hearts turn to their school home to know where and by whom such prayer was offered?

CHAPTER XII.

Fifth and Sixth Years, Continued.

MISS LYON'S EARLY INTEREST IN MISSIONS — LABORS TO KINDLE A LIKE INTEREST AMONG HER PUPILS — THE TRUE STANDARD OF GIVING — THE PRACTICE OF THE JEWS — MEETING OF THE A. B. C. F. M. IN 1842 — HER TEACHERS BECOMING MISSIONARIES — CONTRIBUTIONS — PERSONAL RESPONSIBILITY — SUBJECTS FOR MEDITATION AND PRAYER.

WE have seen that Miss Lyon's first Christian desires were for a world lying in wickedness; and how, from year to year, these desires grew; and how she realized more and more that fellowship with Christ in his sufferings, and this alone, will carry to all the inhabitants of the earth that salvation, the basis of which was laid in tears of blood and groans of the tenderest compassion. But there was a missionary interest in her heart even before she was a Christian; for she said to her school in December, 1842: "Some of the brightest visions of my childhood are of Carey and those who first carried the gospel to the heathen." She adds: "I well remember the time when the names of Mills and his associates began to fall on my ear; I remember the thoughts of my young heart when the subject of foreign missions first began to find its way into the family circle, and to be spoken of as one of the marvelous things of the age. I delight to go over the history of the A. B. C. F. M., the first, the corner-stone of our voluntary benevolent associations. I love the very thought that I can remember the beginnings of this great and glorious enterprise. I beheld the infant rocked in its cradle. I knew not why it was born or wherefore it was there. I have seen it grow, become endowed with understanding, and give laws to other minds and direction to other powers. I remember well my feelings when I heard in my early home that our first missionaries had sailed from Philadelphia and Salem. I honored the spirit that led them forth, reverenced the God they served, and asked, shall I ever be in fuller sympathy with him and with them? Years passed by; and one* went from my native hills, saying, with Paul, 'Behold, I go bound in the spirit to Jerusalem, not knowing the things that shall befall me there.' A tenderer chord was now touched; for I had begun to love the Saviour, and my spirit went forth with his to Jerusalem.

"And so I watched from afar off the departure of each company of our missionaries, and knew as far as I might the history of this Foreign Missionary Society. I have

* Rev. Pliny Fisk.

loved to stand in its inner temple rather than its outer court. I have admired it as I have understood its noble principles, been familiar with its history, and had occasion to thank God for the men whom he has raised up to guide in its counsels, and carry forward its work at home, as well as those who have taken their lives in their hands, and gone forth glad exiles from their country, their kindred, and their father's house. In this society I have found one of my richest fields of thought, of meditation, and of feeling. If I am permitted to behold but one more public scene of moral sublimity, let that be another annual meeting of the American Board. Let me again behold those kindred spirits from all parts of the country and from all departments of business, assembling with one accord, in one place, that they may consult together and transact business in this great cause. Let me listen to their deliberations till my thoughts gain unwonted strength, and my heart an unwonted refreshing. I can never forget our last meeting in Norwich. It was called a little heaven on earth; but to me it seemed more like a scene on a vast platform raised over that 'great gulf fixed,' which no one can pass if he would. On the right was the world of glory, and on the left the world of despair. At one time our attention was directed to the right, and there was but a step between us and heaven, and we sung with new delight: —

'Why was I made to hear thy voice
And enter while there's room,
When thousands make a wretched choice,
And rather starve than come?'

"At another time our attention was directed to the left, and we beheld beneath our feet an innumerable company of immortal beings crowded together and plunging over its awful brink. Ah! we felt then that we could never again seek to please ourselves, and never again forget the cause for which Christ suffered and died. Who among us, in the growth of his mind and in the development of his heart, does not feel himself indebted to the American Board? Who, that knows what it is to have an expanding and deepening Christian sympathy in his bosom, does not in this also feel himself indebted to the American Board? And who can bear the thought of one retrograde step in all its movements? Who would not sooner give his last mite and divide his last loaf? Though the barrel of meal be ever so low, and the cruse of oil be ever so far spent, who will not run and first make a little cake for this servant of the Lord?

"There is not a day in which I do not ask how can I enlighten the understanding, and direct the feelings of my pupils aright on this great subject, the salvation of the world? The trial of giving of my little is nothing in comparison with my anxiety on this point.

And an important part of your work hereafter may be to lead others to give as they should. I fear I can not do for you what I would in one short year.

"What I have said of the American Board applies to other societies laboring in this great work. I look upon our Home and Foreign Missionary, Bible and Tract Societies, as the four corner-stones on which our operations rest. And the question with me is not so much to which evangelical denomination we shall give, as how shall we so unite our efforts as to carry forward most rapidly this work?"

When Miss Lyon uttered these words, she had been for five years in the Mt. Holyoke Seminary. The original building had been enlarged, so that the number of pupils had been increased to about two hundred. Revival had followed revival; but she feared lest they were not doing all they ought to do for the kingdom of Christ. It had been her desire that the seminary should possess the missionary spirit in the highest degree, — a school where all should be trained to live for the saving of a world. She said: "Our hearts must take in the whole world, if we would labor aright for Christ." In labor, prayer, and giving, she remembered the whole world, so we loved to hear her speak such words as these, which she gave us soon after the above: "There are two reasons why we ought to give, — it is right, and it will do good. Thus it is in God's government. He is guided by absolute right and infinite benevolence. The manner in which we act this year is like investing capital. Its influence will be increasing from year to year. There is a standard of giving for every individual. We ought to give what the Lord would have us give. And this we are to find out. If it were written on the walls of our rooms how large or how small a sum we should give, we should not be treated as moral agents.

"We are placed here to live for a little while and then go away and live in another world. How shall we live, and how shall we use what God has given us? He has a plan for every farthing he has placed in our hands. If we are willing and obedient, we may know his plan; but no one will know how much he ought to give, unless he has a strong desire to know. God will make our treasures, whether few or many, a touchstone, — a test of the willingness of our hearts. He has committed to us these earthly treasures, requiring a part to be devoted to spiritual purposes. He might have so supplied all that there would have been no opportunity for us to give; but he has seen it best for us to divide our treasures with others. The Bible is our guide in this, and when it makes known our duty, we are not to answer again. If God asks a part of our pittance, we must not inquire how we can get along without it.

"Our standard of giving must be different from that of those who have gone before us. The lowest of us ought to rise as high as the highest did thirty years ago. We ought to rise as much higher than our parents, as we are younger. We cast no reflections on them. They will receive a crown if they labored and gave according to their light. We have greater light and greater opportunities to do good. The providence of God is opening to the Christian every where a way, a highway, a way of holiness, in which his willing feet may run, as on the wings of the wind, carrying the tidings of salvation to the remotest corners of the earth. It is a privilege to give even the widow's mite. I want you to meet all your treasures in heaven. But remember that riches may be corrupted. We shall find that they have been in the last great day. We shall there find garments moth-eaten, gold and silver cankered, and rust that will eat flesh as fire. But, my dear pupils, you may sell all that you have and give alms, and you will find a treasure in heaven. And oh, what a treasure it will be! — redeemed souls carried to heaven through your instrumentality!

"This sordid money, what is it? Why, we may perhaps keep it till we go to the grave, and then we must give it up. This dust, what is it? God suffers us to show by it how much we love him. He has thus put his stamp upon it; so it has become very precious. Yes, we can give it to Christ, and so secure a never-failing treasure in heaven."

A little later, the subject was pursued by reading passages of Scripture showing the connection between doing and giving in this life and the results in eternity. "We should judge of the pleasure which any thing affords, not by the present delight, but by the remembrances it will bring; and these, to be truly delightful, must be increasingly joyous through time and eternity. Sin has blinded us to the effects of much that we do; but our acts will be to us none the less sources of never-ending joy and woe. We must not be careless of what we have, but remember that God's blessing depends, in no small degree, on the manner we use what he has committed to us for his cause. Pardon is not to be purchased by our contributions; but when the gift of grace is secured, the precious casket may be filled with enduring treasures. There is much in the Bible to establish the belief that a certain proportion of our property should be devoted to the Lord's service. In the Old Testament the system of tithing is fully explained. The clearer light which shines in the New discloses our duty without any need of specific direction. Malachi's words seem to have reference to this subject. The tithes must be given if we would secure the blessing. It seems probable that the Jews gave at least four-tenths of their income. Shall we, under the gospel dispensation, with increased light and increased ability, do less? The Jews all gave, the rich and the poor; and we should count it a privilege that we may do a little if we can not do much. How the Saviour honored the two mites of her who gave *all* her living! The Bible teaches us to give a portion of our income to the Lord, and we must give it before we expend any thing for ourselves. I should not dare to take from that part to give to the common poor, to educate a sister or niece. The work of the world's conversion must not stop for such objects as these. If any class is exempt from giving the specified amount, it is ministers and educated men, whose efforts in other ways are an equivalent.

"When Nehemiah first returned to Jerusalem, the Jews were very poor, but still they gave their tenths before using any for themselves. In Hezekiah's day what a blessing came with their giving! God requires us to give without great ability. We should consider our circumstances, decide what proportion we will give, and adhere to it. I regard it my duty to carry out in my own course of action what I have said to you. You will probably see it all true at the judgment, and may be in the light of eternity will find that I have fallen far below the true standard. Let us make no exceptions in our own favor, but rather, like Paul, make exceptions against ourselves."

Another day of the same month she made the following remarks under this general head: "Benevolent objects assume different garbs. There are societies whose work must be planned months and years beforehand. Our home and foreign missionary societies must pledge support to those whom they send out. We should be very careful not to have our contributions diverted from such objects even for a single year. Let us never go backward one step in such a work as this, but rather onward to the day of our death. If our parents are not benevolent, let us seek to supply their lack of service.

"Practice would not be so diverse in respect to Christian liberality, if the hearts of all were right. Two Christians of equal means would not then be found, one giving five dollars and the other five hundred. This contributing is the current money of the heart. It shows to an extent how much we love. And oh, what a privilege, by giving money, to show our love to Him who has redeemed us! Unto us who are the least of all. The Jews enjoyed a great privilege in being permitted to build an earthly temple; we are permitted to build a spiritual temple. If you have any desire to do good, act at once. In waiting, you may lose the little desire you have. These passive impressions are exceedingly dangerous. Feeling without action brings no reward. Do and suffer, deny yourselves for Christ, and you will count it all joy in the end. I am saying what I wish you to remember when you are far hence and see me no more. May you remember it when I am laid in my grave."

One morning more closed the remarks of that series: "I have but a few words more. Before we take up our contribution, let us all take time, before God, to consider the worth of a single soul. Perhaps we can better understand this by trying to think what it would be for our souls to be lost. When we tremble in view of the possibility of being lost ourselves, then let us do what is assigned to us for other souls that are to exist just as long as we shall exist. Have we ever given and toiled and prayed for those in darkness till we felt the sacrifice? Are you ready to go yourself to the corners of the earth for the salvation of others? If we send others to endure the toils, shall we not be willing to practice self-denial? Do you desire in agony of heart to know what you ought to do? Then give in proportion to your feeling. I often look forward to that day when we shall hear it said: 'Inasmuch as ye did it not unto one of the least of these.' Let us do it unto Christ, and first of all give him our hearts. I seem sometimes to look out through the crevices of my prison-house, and see something of the work given us to do here. And, young ladies, you may see more than I see, and do more than I have done. I love to think that my precious daughters will do for Christ's kingdom what I have not done and fear I never shall do."

At the meeting of the American Board at Norwich, in the autumn of 1842, to which reference has been made, Miss Lyon was deeply impressed with the thought that the seminary must possess more of the missionary spirit. She gathered around her many of her former pupils, who were present, and they prayed that the year just opening might be one of a marked awakening of the missionary spirit. She said: "The seminary was founded to advance the missionary cause. I sometimes feel that our walls were built from the funds of our missionary boards. Certainly much of the money expended upon them was given by those who hold every thing sacred to the Lord, and who, probably, would otherwise have devoted it to sending the gospel directly to the heathen." With such sentiments in their hearts, she, and those with her, prayed, giving the seminary anew to the Lord, and to the missionary work. The Lord accepted the offering, but, in so doing, asked not only that they should give gold and silver, but that one half of the twelve teachers who were with her that year should sooner or later go in person to the heathen. Miss Lyon was often heard to say in subsequent years: "I little knew how much that prayer-meeting would cost me." She had not expected to be called upon to give up those to whom she looked for help in carrying on her work.

Jan. 11th of that year, she said: "Most ladies can doubtless do more for the missionary cause at home than abroad. Here we can, and we will pray, and let us do all we can for the conversion of the world. Give your cordial support not only to the American Board, but to other societies whose great object is to save the world. Wives, mothers, and daughters have much to do to elevate the standard of liberality in those they love. Perhaps, as daughters, you should not be willing to have so much lavished upon you, while there is so little given for the cause of Christ. By constant well doing, you may influence a brother or sister to consecrate all to the cause of benevolence. You may even lead a brother to give himself to the work." She then referred to the little daily prayer-meetings, where the different portions of the world were remembered in prayer, and the laborers in each mentioned by name. She hoped that many more would find time to attend these meetings, and a heart to pray in them. She closed by saying: "When you pray, remember that every lost soul would consider it a happy exchange from the misery of damnation to all the sufferings of every individual from Adam to the end of time, and you are praying for those hastening to such a state."

Three days later, she came into school to say: "I

have said much to you this year upon cherishing a missionary spirit, but very little upon giving yourselves personally to the work abroad. We are now asked for two, to go as teachers to a distant land." She dwelt upon the request with much feeling, and asked all to pray that "the Lord would show us whom he would send."

We pass over weeks, in which she sought to know the Lord's will, to find her at the hour of midnight, Feb. 18th, entering a widowed mother's home, and that mother's daughter by her side. A month before, that mother had said: "If my child thinks that she *must* go, she will go, and I shall probably go soon to my grave." No daughter, who realizes that her mother's heart is in a heavenly Father's hand, would thus go forth. Miss Lyon, too, had said: "I think this is of the Lord. Another will be found, while you will love the seminary more dearly than ever, and may do your missionary work here." But another was not found, and therefore this meeting at that midnight hour. The errand needed no explanation, for it was understood, and few were the words spoken that night. In the morning, the language of the weeping mother was: "Who am I, that I should keep back my child, when my Lord calls for her?" Miss Lyon drew near to say to that mother: "I came with your daughter, because I thought I almost knew your feelings. I give up a daughter also. I have supposed she might comfort you in your declining years, and have her home also with me at the same time, and labor for our dear seminary with me till I go home. If we are to give her up, we shall, in so doing, understand as never before the gift of the Son of God." Ten days later, that daughter left her mother, and closed her labors with Miss Lyon to find her home, her work, and her rejoicing over souls saved in a distant land.*

In that Norwich covenant, Miss Lyon had assured the Lord that she wished the seminary to be wholly consecrated to him. In tender mercy he remembered the word of his handmaiden. He saved many souls, and allowed her to seal her covenant by giving up her teachers. As she bade farewell to one after another, she said: "We love that cause best for which we suffer most." And we are told that she said to the widowed mother of whom we have spoken, at the midnight hour: "I thought I knew something of self-denial in giving money, but I am thankful that I had something else to give; for there is an inner soul that was not then reached." These removals of teachers were so numerous that she was sorely taxed, and her friends sometimes feared that she would sink under them. But they were for a cause she truly loved, and of which she had said: "If I have two idols, they are

* The person here referred to was Miss Fiske. — Ed.

this seminary and the missionary cause; and these were both God's before they were mine." She could give to God and say: "It is easiest, safest, and sweetest to trust him."

There has been an allusion to missionary contributions taken up in the school. These were customary from the beginning, Miss Lyon giving as her reason for it, that "practice will make a more lasting impression on the mind than any amount of instruction. Wherever we are we should consider our missionary contribution a part of our expenses, and plan accordingly." Miss Lyon gave a large portion of her little income, contributing, for several years before her death, no less than ninety dollars each year, from her salary of two hundred, to home and foreign missions. She did not say that others ought to do as she did, but with such an example, her instructions never fell powerless. During the year on which we have been dwelling, the sum of nine hundred and fourteen dollars was contributed to home and foreign missions, and in a later year the amount went up to more than twelve hundred dollars. From 1842 to 1849, no less than seven thousand dollars were thus given.

It was at that time customary for Miss Lyon to have two missionary subscriptions in the course of the year. She brought the subject before the school a second time after this revival, and wrote out her thoughts before giving them to her pupils. They were, about that time, embodied in a little book entitled The Missionary Offering. When it was written, retrenchment in our missions was talked of, and Miss Lyon looked at the sixty recently converted in her school, saying: "How anxious I should be for you, if you were now to be left without Christian watch, and how much more the converts from heathenism must require it!" We subjoin in the Appendix the view of personal responsibility she then gave.*

Miss Lyon not only encouraged her pupils to give for the cause of benevolence, but she sought to help them pray also. On the first Monday in January, 1843, the day set apart for prayer for the conversion of the world, she said to them: "Do you feel that you have no abiding spirit of prayer for missions seek to gain missionary intelligence from week to week, and give an hour, at least, each week, to meditating on some great truth, as the love of Christ, the worth of a soul. This will help you to pray, and you will love to pray."

The following subjects of prayer were given to her school on that day:—

"SUBJECTS FOR MEDITATION AND PRAYER.

"I. *Confession.* Of our sins, individual and particular, before and after conversion. Social sins — here, by ex-

* Appendix, p. 243.

ample — at home. — Enlarge until you confess the sins of the whole world. — Pray for heathen as sinners, not as unfortunate beings. — Think of the guilt of the world.

"II. *Meditate on the atoning blood of Christ.* Dwell upon it, and enlarge as on the preceding topic. — Sin to be the great object of thought, and the atoning blood of Christ is the only corresponding thought.

"III. *Eternal punishment.* Unless we dwell upon this truth we cannot realize the fullness of the atonement. — Pray first for ourselves and then for others. — How many have gone down to everlasting death since we came into this room — since we awoke this morning!

"IV. *Eternal happiness.* Dwell upon eternal happiness in the love of Christ.

"V. *Infinite value of the soul,* and the equal value of all souls.

"PRAY FOR OURSELVES.

"I. Pray for yourself as an individual. — What does God require of you in regard to yourself? — What in relation to your friends, — in relation to the heathen world? What do we need from God that we may do what he requires of us?

"II. For the conversion of souls in our family. — Pray for them on account of their influence in the conversion of the world.

"III. Pray for the continued prevalence of religion in our family.

"PRAY DIRECTLY FOR THE CONVERSION OF THE WORLD.

"I. Dwell on the promises that this world shall be converted.

"II. Pray that the fulfillment of these promises may be hastened. — Think of the truth that it can be hastened by believing prayer, or delayed by the neglect of it. — Pray as though you were the only person in the universe.

"III. Pray for the prevalence of a missionary spirit. — When we pray for the conversion of souls, pray that they may be so converted as to have a missionary spirit.

"IV. Pray for the success of missionary operations.

"V. Pray for a blessing on missionary societies.

"VI. Pray for missionaries themselves.

"VII. Pray for particular missionary stations.

"VIII. Pray for those who have been members of this school and are now missionaries.

"IX. Pray for eminent laborers at home in the missionary work.

"X. Pray for a universal spirit of liberality and a universal spirit of prayer throughout the world."

CHAPTER XIII.

From the Sixth to the Tenth Year.

PROSPERITY OF THE SEMINARY IN 1842 — DEPARTURE OF MISS FISKE TO PERSIA — RELIGIOUS SORROW — REVIVAL OF 1843 — ITS FRUITS — EIGHTH, NINTH, AND TENTH YEARS, 1844 TO 1846 — REVIVAL OF 1846 — DEATH OF REV. MR. CONDIT — DEATH OF MISS WASHBURN.

MISS LYON wrote Mrs. Banister in December, 1842, in regard to her school, as follows: "We have had a very prosperous year in worldly things. Every thing is systematized, and Miss Moore and Miss Whitman urge forward the wheels so beautifully that all seems more than ever like clock-work. I enjoy very much having every thing done better by others than it can be by myself. If this pleasure continues to increase as it has done for a year or two, I hope I may be prepared to be happy in being old and in being laid aside as a useless thing. But in spiritual things we are less favored. There has been less interest than we have had any year since the first. Pray for us that we may not receive all our good things in this life."

Miss Lyon rejoiced in the external prosperity of her school and in the increase of missionary interest; and when one of her teachers* left this year to go in person to the benighted, her whole soul was in the matter, and she was with her day and night to give some of the choicest counsels that ever fell from mortal lips, and to know that every thing was done, that could be done, for her. When the moment of separation came, she whispered a last word of counsel, and then said: "You will pray for us — will you not? — all the way to Persia. As you remember the dear seminary, you can not do otherwise. When you lie in your berth, will you not carry us to God?" A year afterward, she wrote that friend: "It is one year this week since we were in Boston together. I can never forget that week after you left, which I spent there especially to rest, to meditate, and to try to pray; and I can never forget the scenes of the month that followed, — the unspeakable grace of God then manifested. I shall ever regard those scenes as among the most striking in exhibiting and illustrating the great scheme of salvation."

That missionary company embarked March 1, 1843; and Miss Lyon left those departing ones to return to Deacon Safford's, where she had been for several days, o give her time and thoughts to meditation and prayer for her beloved pupils. The hearts of the members of that family were drawn into close communion with

* Miss Fiske.

hers, as she pleaded for a heavenly rain to descend on the dear seminary. She seemed to them like Elijah bowed upon Carmel. We love to think of holy communings which one of that number now has with her in heaven; and those who remain on earth thank God that they were there permitted to have fellowship with her in intercessions for immortal souls. They can not forget how she appeared as she turned from them, March 7th, saying: "Pray, pray for us."

She reached South Hadley just at the time of the afternoon exercise in the seminary hall. She gave the pupils the particulars of the departure of the teacher, and closed by saying: "Young ladies, you have one less to labor for you; but, I trust, none the less to pray for you. The last [illegible] that I said to Miss Fiske was: 'Pray, pray for us.' And, as I watched her till she was lost to my sight, I could but feel that with her last look of her native land she prayed for you. Will you not pray for yourselves?"

She went from the seminary hall to soon gather her teachers around her. One of those teachers wrote Miss Fiske soon after: "At that meeting, Miss Lyon's heart was too full for us to ask her of your last days in Boston. She had told us in school of her request to you on parting; and in repeating it to us, she convinced us that we had a work in our closets. She seemed to be burdened with the thought that prayer is our only refuge in this fearful extremity, and that, if there is not an immediate work, we shall probably lose the blessing. I never felt as when sitting there to hear Miss Lyon ask in almost agony: 'Is there one here to pray?' Teachers went to their rooms in silence with the feeling that their work was alone with God. The next day was our recreation day; and the very silence of our house seemed to fill us with awe. Hearts were too full to pray together much."

Thursday morning, March 9th, Miss Lyon met her school as usual for worship. Mrs. Peabody, of St. Louis, has made the following record of that morning's exercise: "Miss Lyon said that she wished to stay away from us, that she might have an uninterrupted opportunity to think of the present religious state of the family. It was a relief to her feelings that she was not saying any thing to us that would harden our hearts and prove a savor of death unto death. She could pray for us without doing this. But she desired to return that she might find others to pray also. She could not ask any particular individual to pray, any more than when she sought to find the missionary teacher, lest she should not ask the right one. If any had a heart to pray, she did hope they would do so, that we might not separate from one another without a rich blessing. In the ordinary course of events, the first of the year is the period for fixing impressions, —

then is the precious revival season, if at all, usually; and the summer term the time to stamp the last impress for eternity to many. That is the sifting time; the chaff is separated from the wheat; Christians are built up; and those who are not Christians yield to the temptations which then abound."

In the afternoon general exercise, she left the ordinary class of topics, and spoke upon religious sorrow. She said: "We know that there is a connection between religious sorrow and spiritual blessings, though we know not why it is. If there were no need of the blessing, there would be no need of the sorrow. But the Christian must commence his work in sorrow, and it follows him all the way along."

On Friday morning the 10th, Mrs. P. says: "Miss Lyon read the account of Abraham's praying for Sodom; compared it to a weight thrown into a scale, which would have turned in the wicked city's favor if ten righteous persons had been found in it." Oh! how Miss Lyon now watched that suspended scale; and prayer after prayer was cast in till the blessing came most richly. The Sabbath was a day of interest, and when Miss Lyon invited those who had indulged hope since the commencement of the school-year to meet her, fourteen came together. She rejoiced over them, but the burden of her cry was for those out of the ark of safety; and the first time she met her pupils after the Sabbath, it was to speak of Christ sorrowing and praying. Christians felt, as they listened to her, that they were almost strangers to sympathy with Christ in his sorrow for a world. They went away to pray more. Miss Lyon was now partially laid aside from labor, but it was to pray; and though suffering she still met the anxious every day.

The results of the work of grace which followed are given in the following letter to Mrs. Banister: —

"April 13, 1843.

"I hoped I should have quite a large part of this sheet to tell you what the Lord hath wrought for us since I last wrote you. I believe, just at the time that I sent my last letter, a cloud of mercy was gathering over our heads, and a few drops had fallen upon us. The cloud had so long been gathering, and so gently, that we scarcely knew it; but soon the windows of heaven were opened, and the blessing descended, so that there was scarcely room in our minds or hearts to receive it. When I returned from Boston, there were a few more than fifty without hope. In about three weeks, all but six expressed some hope that they had found the Saviour; in a single week of this time, more than thirty of the number.

"In all my privileged experience connected with the work of the Spirit, this, I think, has been of unparalleled rapidity; and yet I have never witnessed more quietness and stillness than in its progress, or any less of what some call *reaction* to be watched against in the result. It has seemed like a sudden, powerful shower bursting upon us, but descending with so much gentleness that not a leaf or twig among the tender plants is turned out of its place, and then so suddenly giving way to the beautiful sun and refreshing dews. But, as teachers, we have a great work to cherish these tender plants. Shall we not have your prayers? Oh, to follow Christ in the work of cherishing them is what I want! This desire enters almost daily into the very depths of my soul with an untold and unwonted strength."

The effects of this revival of 1843 were very marked upon Christians. Some choice spirits went forth to bless the world, and there were many who then received a quickening, which led them to labor most faithfully in the seminary that year and while they were connected with it. An account of a prayer-meeting, written by one of the young ladies at the time, shows something of their feelings. It occurred near the close of the year, and was a meeting at which teachers were not usually present. She says: "In our little Sabbath morning circle Miss Lyon said much of the importance and privilege of having that well of water within us, of which Jesus spake, springing up into eternal life. 'We ought to attain to that standard of piety set before us in the gospel, and ever be enabled to say: "I will do either this or that, whichever may seem most likely to promote God's glory." We may be called to honor him by patient suffering, or in some prominent station, or in some humble, obscure station. But we may have that state of mind in which our first thought in making any change of circumstances will be, not will it promote my own happiness, (God can make any situation happy), but will it be most for God's glory?' The minds of all the circle seemed to have been directed to the attainment of a high degree of holiness, and Miss Lyon remarked that there might be some design of Providence in thus directing our thoughts. And she added: 'It is a means of grace to be accustomed to seek and watch the guidance of Providence.'"

About thirty-five became Christians during this year, and there was a delightful state of religious interest to the close.

The next year, that of 1844–5, by some mistake too many were received, — the house was crowded. There was much external prosperity, but only about twelve hopeful conversions. Much prayer was offered for those out of Christ. One of the teachers in reviewing the year has said: "It was not answered in the conversion of many of the impenitent, but who shall say that it did not avail much? There were blessed restraining influences thrown around us that were entirely from God."

Miss Lyon said of herself, during that year: "My sun has already gone beyond the meridian of my usefulness. I feel that my work is almost done. The effort of raising my voice teaches me that it can continue but a little longer. If I say any thing which will lead you to live such a life as you would wish to live, to die such a death as you would wish to die, and to fit you for such an eternity as you would wish to enjoy, treasure it up. It often seems to me, that I am giving you my last legacy."

A teacher wrote the September after the year closed: "God was merciful to us; for though he sent us so large a number, they were as a school disposed to do right, and to be studious, so that our work was much lightened. The year has been a very pleasant one. We have lacked but one thing, the presence of the Holy Spirit by his converting influences. The blessed effects upon the few who felt his power only made us feel our need the more. It was sad to see so many go away without the love of Christ in their heart. May the Spirit of God follow them! Oh, what a work it is to watch for souls, — to feel that one is exerting an influence upon them for eternity! I think I do desire to do the will of God, — to be found in just the place, and doing just what he appoints. But I can do nothing without the blessing of God. May a rich blessing from him rest upon our school the coming year. If we can have that, it will be enough, whatever else may betide."

Those teachers were observing a concert of prayer during all their long vacation, and asking, to use the words of one of their number, "if they might be counted worthy to once more point souls to Christ." Watching and praying, there came a blessing. The school year opened, and, as early as the first week, the special presence of the Holy Spirit was manifest in the conversion of one of the pupils. During the first term twenty indulged the Christian hope, and about the same number later in the year.

Soon after the close of this year, two of the teachers, Mrs. Howland and Mrs. Webb, left the country for India; another, Mrs. Pitkin, entered the home missionary field, and several of the pupils were about to engage in the same work. After mentioning these facts to her missionary friend in Persia, one of the teachers writes: "Do you not think that dear Miss Lyon's heart glows with sacred joy to bring to the altar so valuable missionary offerings? Her cup of joy was almost full, when for two successive years our contributions amounted to more than one thousand dollars;

but how much more she rejoices to bring her loved and efficient daughters and give them to the work!"

Before twelve months had passed, Miss Lyon was called to make another offering, which touched her heart as no other one had done, and required a large measure of faith and resignation. When the school came together in 1846, the places of three of the teachers of the previous year were occupied by strangers. Mrs. Burgess and Mrs. Hazen were on their way to India, and Mrs. Lord was soon to leave her native land for China. One of these had, for years, stood by Miss Lyon as associate principal, and was considered as almost necessary to the existence of the school, and the others could not easily be spared. Miss Lyon was cheerful in all these changes, but when she told the school of Miss Moore's (Mrs. Burgess) proposal to leave her, she could only compose herself by asking the young ladies to sing, "God moves in a mysterious way."

She wrote Mrs. Banister the following November: "I have passed through many scenes, the last year, of deep and tender interest to me, concentrating the feelings of many years into one, and obviously increasing my gray hairs. I feel the loss of my two nieces socially more than in our business, though both were very important to the school."

We here give a few sentences from her letters to

Mrs. Burgess, in India, which show with what warm affection she followed her friends to their distant homes.

"May 10th, 1847. — Your first letter arrived Saturday evening. I have read it twice with tears and tender interest. There is something peculiar in the feeling of receiving the first. Mr. Condit was here today. I told him that I would lend it to him, though I did not expect to lend the original to but very few, because I wish to keep it just as long as I live. I expect to read it many times when I am musing alone. Your interest in remembering me is a great personal comfort, but not so important a duty for you as many that will have a claim upon you in your new home. As I read your letter, I thought you might like to spell out my blind penmanship now and then, if I should write nothing more than the little things which should occur to me from day to day. So I have begun this sheet, and shall add a little from time to time till it is full.

"It is now vacation. A few days before it commenced, Miss Whitman was called to attend the funeral of her brother's wife. All the other teachers were wishing to go away, and all who have rendered any aid in the care of the domestic department would like to go, too. So I said at once, go. Here I am, lord of all I survey, and the undoubted mistress of all the departments in the establishment. But we have the best family of nearly fifty which could be had. So a kind Providence, which tempers the breeze to the shorn lamb, takes care of me. But I must bid you good-night and go away to sleep. May guardian angels ever watch around your pillow!

"May 21. — We have had a very pleasant vacation, though I have been exceedingly busy. I had considerable done in the line of the work of masons and carpenters, so that I can have more time for rest and journeying in the autumn. One afternoon, I invited the young ladies to a sewing party to repair our church-cushions. As we had no apples, we had oranges and raisins. For amusement, we gave each an opportunity, taking them in order by States, to give some account of their family. Last my turn came. In my account, I told them of my three nephews, that I expect soon to visit me. . . When I write to you and receive your letters, I can not feel that I shall never see you again. But it is but a little, short way to heaven, — short to both of us, and sure, I hope.

"June 15. — I was going to add another sheet to this, but as the journal is going this morning, I will send it as it is. My health all the first part of the year was very far from being good. I suppose I am in danger, — my lungs especially. My excitement about giving up you and Lucy might have done something to lay the foundation. But I have not had the least regret that you have gone, though my heart clings to you with fond and increasing interest. You remember I was not in good health last summer. I can now bear more than I could a year ago. May that life be given to God."

At an earlier date she says: "I have many things to make me remember that my home is not a permanent one here. Last year how many of my kindred were around me! Now all are away save one. But I have no regret. I am altogether reconciled to both your and Lucy's going. The remembrance of the years you both spent with me is precious. The communion with your hearts is still precious, and especially our meeting around the mercy-seat."

Before Miss Moore left the seminary, Miss Lyon wrote as follows to Miss Fiske, in Persia: "You sympathize in *all* the things which are passing among us, and especially in those events which relate to the missionary cause. I know that some of your kind friends will be sure to tell you that Miss Moore is really going. It will surprise you, as it has many here. The first question generally is,—'What does Miss Lyon think of it?' I have nothing to say in all these things, only to ask that the will of the Lord may be done, and to submit to all the dispensations of Providence, whether with or without means to carry out our plans. This is certainly a great event to us, especially to me. My only wish concerning it is, that it may be for the furtherance of the gospel. We know so little of the great plans of God, that it is wisest and safest and sweetest to leave all with him."

Miss Lyon did leave all with him, though at the commencement of the school year in October every thing in regard to the seminary looked very dark. She was herself laid aside by ill-health. Miss Moore was absent, and Miss Whitman's heart sank within her, as she looked upon the burden of responsibility thus rolled upon her; but she, too, could look upward, assured that might would be increased to one that had no strength. He in whom they trusted did not disappoint them. Miss Lyon was able to speak to the school but few times during the first term. Rev. Mr. Hawks conducted the daily morning exercises, and Rev. Mr. Condit, the pastor of the church in the village, with his usual readiness to aid, came into the seminary, and attended a meeting on Thursday evening, for several weeks, embracing the whole school. The labors of these gentlemen were very acceptable to the young ladies, and were much blessed. When the religious interest commenced, there were ninety not Christians in the family; sixty of these had just entered the institution, and thirty had been under Miss Lyon's instruction, some for one and others for two years. The coming of the Spirit was like a rushing, mighty wind.

At the first meeting for inquirers, which was held the second week in December, nineteen were present. In a few days, the interest became so deep and general that it seemed impossible to give the usual attention to lessons, and a day was set apart for fasting and prayer. In less than two weeks sixty were rejoicing in a newly-found Saviour. A band of youthful Christians from the middle class were particularly zealous in their prayers and efforts for their impenitent companions; and their labors were not in vain. Miss Lyon lived but two years after this revival, always to keep fresh the memory of "that precious middle class."

About this time, a teacher of much promise was obliged to leave, on account of failing health; and after passing a few weeks with her friends, she entered the mansions above. Miss Lyon had anticipated much from her, and mourned her early death; but, with her usual spirit of submission, she said: "I feel that it is a blessed privilege to fit dear ones for heaven;" and added, while the tears coursed down her cheeks: "I thank God that I have not yet heard of the death of any pupil of this beloved seminary without hope in Jesus. If any have thus died, I have been spared the trial of hearing of it."

The second term found Miss Lyon's health improved; but still she was not able to take the entire charge of the religious exercises. As she met her school January 22, she told them, that while she could not speak to them every day, she intended, as her strength might permit, to take up "the Christian's duty and privilege in regard to the conversion of the world." It seemed to her providential that she had been unable to take up the subject before; for now many hearts, that would have been uninterested, would feel very differently.

The year 1846 closed with twenty still wanting the Christian hope.

During the vacation, Miss Lyon was deprived of the counsel and society of a long-tried friend by the death of Rev. Mr. Condit. He had been the pastor of the church in the village during all her residence in South Hadley, and had ever stood by her, sympathizing with her and giving her aid in her trials and perplexities, and participating in her joy in the prosperity of her school. She thus speaks of his sickness, in a letter to Mrs. Burgess, dated September 10: "From the sadness of my heart I must write you a few lines this evening. Our dear Mr. Condit is very near his home in heaven You have doubtless been informed of his feeble health the summer past. He has not been able to preach, — has been to church but one half day for many months. I have seen him twice since my return from New Marlboro'. The king of terrors is approaching with slow and gentle step, as if loth to take his prey; but he approaches nearer and nearer. Here I am alone in this great building; no one near to interrupt my grief. I love even this solitude for my tears and my prayers in his behalf. The years of our acquaintance pass in rapid review before my mind. As I dwell on him as a friend, a Christian, a counselor, a pastor, sadness spreads a dark pall over my whole soul. And yet it is not all sorrow. Heaven seems to be opening her gates in waiting readiness to receive another servant of Christ, another redeemed soul, another glorified saint into its blest abode."

The year 1847–8 passed pleasantly and prosperously. The changes which Miss Moore's departure made necessary had been effected. Miss Lyon's health had improved so that she was able to be in school regularly. The influence of the revival of the previous year was favorably felt in the consistent lives of the converts; and cases of seriousness among the impenitent early occurred. Between fifty and sixty found hope in the mercy of Christ during the year; and Miss Lyon remarked near its close that "the Holy Spirit had never tarried so long with them by his converting influences." In May of this year Miss Lyon was called to stand by the dying bed of one of her pupils and cheer her by pointing to Christ as she went down to the dark valley. The following letter to Mrs. Porter gives a brief account of the circumstances: —

"South Hadley, May 28, 1848.

"Now I must tell you of the dealings of our heavenly Father with us. Death has again entered our family, and taken home one of the dear lambs of Christ's fold. The attending circumstances relating to this world were rather peculiarly trying; but to another world they were all consoling, comforting, joyful. The dear one was Emily Washburn, daughter of Rev. Mr. Washburn, of Suffield, Conn., seventeen years of age, a most lovely character and exemplary Christian. She was almost the idol of her devoted parents. One week ago last Wednesday she attended the recess meeting and led in prayer; and the next Wednesday morning, at four o'clock, she entered heaven, as we trust. Thus rapid were the ravages of death. Her parents were away on a journey. The intelligence could not reach them so that they could arrive before her death. A particular friend of theirs came on, as soon as he learned of her sickness, and stayed and took home the remains. They were sent away by railroad at twelve o'clock of the same day. From that time till Friday noon, I can not tell you how my heart trembled, at every ringing of the bell, at the anticipated meeting with the father and mother. Friday noon, the mother arrived. She hastened in the public conveyance before her husband, as he was with his own carriage. God helped me to tell her, and sustained her under the stroke. I will some time tell you of the precious words and last prayer of the dying one. When asked what message she would leave for her father and mother, she said: 'Tell them that Jesus called me, and I could not wait for them; for Christ says, "He that loveth father or mother more than me is not worthy of me."' So grace has again triumphed over sin, and another redeemed spirit has gone home."

The morning after Miss Washburn's death, Miss Lyon's theme, in addressing the school, was the great salvation. She spoke of the difficulty she always found in communicating any just views on this subject, and added: "No one knows how often or how greatly I have been bowed down with this burden, so that I could only exclaim, 'Oh that God would speak!' and now he has spoken to us. It is not so much a voice of warning addressed to us, as an invitation; not a voice from the *tomb*, but from *heaven*. We have been led very near to heaven; the very gates have been opened, and are now scarcely shut. Through them we have been permitted to see Jesus. He has himself, through one of his members, been speaking to us in melting tones of persuasion and love. He has given us an impressive lesson on his great salvation. And now I entreat you, 'give heed to the things you have heard, lest at any time you should let them slip.' "

Many of the extracts from Miss Lyon's letters show with what tender sympathy she entered into the feelings of those in affliction. We give here a letter from Mrs. Porter, which speaks more fully of this trait in her character: " Learning, while in Boston last week, that reminiscences of Miss Mary Lyon were being recorded, my thoughts have reverted much to the thirteen years I was favored with an intimate acquaintance with this dear, faithful follower of Jesus.

" Others will speak of her superior powers of mind, her intellectual attainments, the Bible type of her piety, aptness for imparting instruction, and great business talents; but my mind dwells more especially on the sympathizing qualities of her heart. It is so seldom these traits are combined with great energy of character, a ruling mind, and the designing and accomplishing plans of magnitude, that it was the impression of many, not intimately acquainted with Miss Lyon, that she might be deficient in gentleness and appreciation of the sorrows and feebleness of others. It is a great mistake. Two years after our first introduction to Miss Lyon, death was commissioned to enter our family and take from us a daughter thirteen years of age, — the last of four children. Miss Lyon had been much in our family for a year and a half, and knew what she was to us. In the large circle of relatives and friends who sympathized so deeply with us in this sore bereavement, none seemed more affectionately, sincerely, softly to come into the depths of the sorrows of our stricken hearts, than Miss Lyon.

"In other cases I have repeatedly witnessed her tender sympathy. When her beloved pastor, Mr. Condit, was borne to the grave, how did her flowing tears evince the fountain of grief in her soul; and how was the bereaved widow cared for, and sympathized with in the tenderest manner. Once I called with her on an aged clergyman, with whom she was but slightly acquainted, who had recently buried a lovely daughter on whom he leaned much for support. The readiness with which she entered into his sorrows, and sought to direct his mind to sources of consolation, impressed my mind deeply, as I knew that just at that time she was unusually burdened with cares and perplexities relative to her beloved institution. 'Do you not think, dear sir,' said she, 'that we should reflect much on the goodness of God, that these severe cases of discipline and grief are the rare exceptions, and not the general experience, of our lives? Death, I learn, has repeatedly entered your family and removed those most dear; but how many years of prosperity have passed between those scenes! Then, and but a little while and in a brighter world, all this will be rejoiced over, when we see fully that it was all ordered in the best time and manner."

"In no case was sympathy ever expressed because circumstances seemed to require it, but to flow forth from a full soul, that 'mourned with those that mourned.' The permanent invalid found in her one that could realize how severe the affliction of protracted debility and disease, and receive from her the most considerate attention and sympathy. What watchful care she would uniformly exercise when in our family to relieve me of any exertion on her account, saying frequently: 'If I can not bear your burdens, do let me add to them as little as possible.' At times she would gently press in her hands my aching head and say: 'I fear you will never have a better head on earth, but in heaven the "head will be no more sick nor the heart faint." Your kind heavenly Father knows just how much it is best you should suffer here.''

CHAPTER XIV.

Sickness and Death.

DECLINING HEALTH — HER RELINQUISHMENT OF HOUSE-KEEPING CARES — VISIT TO MONSON — SICKNESS AND DEATH OF MISS W. — LAST ADDRESS TO HER SCHOOL — HER ILLNESS AND WEAKNESS — VISIT OF REV. MR. SWIFT — COMMENCEMENT OF DELIRIUM — HER LAST WORDS — DEATH — FUNERAL — PROGRESS OF THE SEMINARY SINCE MISS LYON'S DECEASE.

FROM Miss Lyon's frequent allusions to the shortness of life, in her advancing years, it would seem as if she realized that the work her Master had for her here on the earth was nearly accomplished; but to her friends she appeared to have the prospect of years of usefulness before her. With the exception of a little deafness, the hand of time rested lightly upon her, and she entered with as much life and energy into whatever was brought before her as in her younger years. As the house-keeping department was a peculiar feature in her institution, she desired to make the conveniences for it as complete as possible. This led her repeatedly to alter the arrangements of the domestic hall, and so frequently had it been done that it had become a subject of remark with some of her friends. During the vacation in the months of August and September of 1848, the workmen were kept very busy in that room, and it was essentially remodeled.

When her teachers returned, at the commencement of the school year, Miss Lyon took them down to the room, one after another, and showed them what had been done. After explaining the reasons for her alterations, she said: "These arrangements are now as perfect as I can make them. I shall never change them again. My time and strength are now to be given more fully to the literary department."

She gave over the house-keeping cares as she had never before done, and professedly turned her attention to the studies of her pupils; but in reality their spiritual interests occupied the larger portion of her thoughts. Miss Whitman's failing health compelled her to seek rest soon after the school was organized, and, with only the younger teachers to aid her, an unusual burden of care rested upon Miss Lyon; but strength was given her to meet it. Her health was good, and never did she manifest more enthusiasm in her plans for the improvement of her pupils, never did she present truth with more life and power, never with more unction and pathos than during this winter. She noticed this increased vigor, and one day said to some of her teachers: "I don't know why it is that my mind is so active. It sometimes seems to me that I am doing my last work."

At the close of the first term, she went to Monson to spend the vacation of two weeks with Mr. and Mrs. Porter. Of this visit, Mrs. Porter gives the following interesting account: —

"When at the seminary on the Thanksgiving occasion previous to her death, I said to Miss Lyon: 'You know an invitation to spend your vacations with us is stereotyped; may we not expect you in the winter vacation?' She replied: 'I think I shall come previous to vacation, and rest, for *circles* are so broken up then, that it is more difficult getting along than in the term time.' She came, however, in that vacation; and, the first evening after she arrived, she told me, 'that what decided her to come after concluding she should remain at the seminary during vacation was, she had never felt the responsibility of giving religious instruction as this winter. Oh, when I come before those young immortals to teach them eternal truths, I am borne down with a sense of its importance as never before, and I wanted to come to my *resting-home*' (as she was wont to call our house), 'where, in that quiet chamber, I could seek anew for wisdom, grace, and strength for the great work.'

"The teachers, she said, were very urgent she

should go to New York to sit for her portrait, — so much so, that she was reluctant not to comply with their kind request, and accept of their generous offer to bear all the expense. 'But to me,' she added, 'it seemed of so little consequence to have my picture taken, compared with seeking a better preparation for my important duties, that I could not comply.'

"Every thing in her conversation and appearance indicated a 'fresh anointing.' All business with regard to the seminary was laid aside. Previously, she had invariably come with account books, and a list of various items of business to consult Mr. Porter about; and, as soon as he came in, business was the theme. Now she introduced no subject of business but twice during her stay, and one of those times said but a few words.

"Mr. Porter said to me on Sabbath eve (she came the Friday previous), 'Does not Miss Lyon seem unusually spiritual?' I replied, 'I think so, evidently; I never saw her so heavenly-minded.' Little did I then think she was pluming her wings for her upward flight. She appeared as well as I ever saw her, and repeatedly spoke with gratitude of her excellent health. At our dinner-table, a day or two previous to her leaving, she remarked, playfully, 'Mr. Porter, you and Mrs. Porter have been afraid I should break down at the seminary, but' (dropping her knife and fork, and straightening up), 'Do you not think I am in pretty good trim? I have an excellent appetite; I sleep like a child, and have none of that chilliness I have had when rather exhausted with my labors. I feel quite vigorous.' We both told her we thought we had not seen her better, and the conclusion of us all was, that she had as good a prospect of physical ability to labor on at the seminary for ten years to come as for the past ten years.

"When she left us, I felt, more than ever before, that it was a rare privilege to enjoy her personal friendship, and have her so frequently an inmate of our family. Ever since my first acquaintance with Miss Lyon, I had thought I had never seen the blessed principles and precepts of the gospel of Christ so strikingly exemplified in any of his professed followers. But on account of her active business habits, and constantly planning for improvements in her beloved seminary, I had not seen exhibited that contemplative, devotional state of mind which was developed in this visit. There was evinced an absorbing love to the Lord Jesus; Christ was her theme, and the privilege of laboring for him, and making sacrifices for his cause, dwelt on much. I think I have never witnessed a nearer approach to the mercy-seat than was apparent in social prayer just before leaving. It was almost the last sound of her voice I ever heard."

While thus seeking after intimate communion with her Saviour, and new views of his love, that she might be more successful in her efforts to win sinners to his fold, she was putting her house in order, and preparing to enter into fullness of joy and blessedness with him. Three weeks after the school assembled for the second term of the year, Miss W., a pupil from Ware, N. H., died under trying circumstances. She had been confined to her room for a few days by influenza, then quite prevalent in school, but had so far recovered as to be able to go out to her recitations, when her sickness returned, assuming the form of malignant erysipelas. The disease made rapid progress, so that Miss Lyon had only just learned that her pupil was again sick, when it was told her that she could, probably, live but a short time.

Miss Lyon was suffering at the time from influenza and a severe nervous headache, and was in the right state to feel most keenly the trying nature of her position. She hastened to the bedside of her dying pupil, regardless of exposure to her disease; spoke words of comfort to her, and bent over her to catch, if possible, her replies. Then the painful intelligence must be communicated to Miss W.'s parents who had not as yet heard of her first illness. The next day was the last Thursday in February, — the fast for literary institutions; a day that had been looked forward to with earnest solicitude that it might be blessed to the family. With these anxieties upon her mind, Miss Lyon passed a sleepless night, and was able to say but a few words to her school on Thursday.

On Friday she was better. Miss W. still lingered in an unconscious state; but there was much excitement among the pupils from the sudden approach of death, and the fearful disease that had appeared in the midst of them. Miss Lyon met her school both morning and afternoon, and spoke to them her last precious words, — words which seemed at the time to come from one upon whom the beams of heavenly light were already shining. She entreated her pupils with great earnestness to turn their thoughts from the things about them, and follow the dying one up to the "celestial city, and, as its pearly gates opened to receive her, look in and catch a glimpse of its glories." With a rapture not of earth she exclaimed: "Oh, if it were I, how happy I should be to go!" but added: "Not that I would be unclothed while I can do any thing for you, my dear children." She spoke to the impenitent in an impressive manner, saying, with great tenderness: "If one of you were on that dying bed, I could not take your hand and go with you down to that world of despair. It would be too painful for me. I should feel that I must draw the veil and leave you." She besought them to make the Saviour their friend at once, not because they feared death, but because he is a being of such infinite perfection.

She read passages from the Bible, which speak of the fear of God, and remarked upon them. She looked upon all anxiety about the future as distrust of our kind heavenly Father, and asked: "Shall we fear what he is about to do?" adding, with great emphasis: "There is nothing in the universe that I fear, but that I shall not know all my duty, or shall fail to do it."

That evening, which was the last time she met her pupils for family prayers, she read 2 Corinthians v. She went from the table very soon to meet the sorrowing father and give him the painful details of his daughter's illness, — then to go with him to that daughter's side, and see the happy look of recognition and unsuccessful effort to speak. Before midnight the spirit had entered the realms of bliss. Miss Lyon had earnestly desired that the father might arrive while his child was yet living, and now said she was "so filled with gratitude to God for his goodness in this respect that she could not rest."

She again passed a sleepless night, and met her school at five o'clock in the morning, when they gathered for prayers, before the remains of their companion should be taken away. This was the last time her voice was heard in the school-room. She then read the hymn commencing —

"Why do we mourn departed friends,"

saying that it was the best expression she could give of her feelings.

She spent Saturday quietly in her room, sleeping much of the time, and at evening appeared refreshed; but the mail brought her the sad intelligence of the death of a nephew by suicide, without leaving evidence of his being a Christian. This was an overwhelming blow to her, and the night was one of deep sorrow and anguish. On Sabbath morning she was so much worse that she could not sit up, and medical advice was sought. She was very much prostrated, and could make little mental effort, but she desired the friends who sat with her through the day to read very slowly hymns or passages of Scripture, stopping at the end of each line, that she might repeat it and so take in the meaning. Many hours were spent in thus reading the Psalms or the precious hymns in the book entitled "Songs in the Night." When any thing of special interest to her occurred, she would repeat it several times.

Monday morning found her still worse, and it was evident to the anxious friends watching by her side that the dreaded erysipelas had fastened itself upon her. It was not of the malignant type, but her peculiar temperament, her constitution, her past labors, and the nervous excitement from which she was suffering when taken, made the case one of great danger. This she fully realized, but it caused her no anxiety. Giving up her solicitude for her family, she occupied herself as she was able with thoughts of her preparation for what might be before her. She desired that there might be no more change in her attendants than was necessary; that only those should be allowed to come into her room who had the care of her; and, prompted by a natural aversion to being gazed upon from curiosity, added that it would distress her exceedingly, at any time, to look up and see several persons standing in the doorway or about the room, though they might be very dear friends. At one time, she desired pencil and paper to be brought, that she might dictate some of her thoughts in regard to the school, should she not recover; at another, to leave some message for a nephew in whom she had felt a deep interest; but in both cases was so overpowered by her disease as to be able to give but one sentence. She was peaceful and happy, often repeating, "The will of the Lord be done: I desire to be spared only to labor for him."

On Tuesday afternoon, Rev. Mr. and Mrs. Swift, of Northampton, called to see her, at her request. After a little conversation with him, she desired Mr. Swift to read a short portion of Scripture, a few words at a time, allowing her to repeat after him, and pray.

When Mrs. Swift went to her bedside, she grasped her hand and said: "It is good to look at you." She spoke of her sufferings, and remarked that the physicians hoped for a favorable issue, but it was doubtful; and added that the crisis was near, and if the result was unfavorable, she had very little time left in which she should be able to think. "Now," said she, "I want to tell you how it is, that you may *then* pray for me. If I ever get to heaven, it will be the greatest miracle of grace. I am so unworthy, — *so unworthy*." And then, brightening up, she said: "I *rejoice* to be unworthy, and to owe it all to the atoning blood of Jesus Christ." She might have said more, but much was depending upon her being kept very quiet, and it was not thought best to tempt her to tax her strength further. After Mrs. Swift had repeatedly expressed the fear that she would weary herself, she said: "Well, I will not finish the sentence," and bade her good-by.

A few hours more, and delirium came on. The force of the disease which had prostrated her seemed to be subsiding on Thursday morning; but the excitement of the brain increased, and congestion followed. The three ensuing days were very painful ones, not only to the sufferer, but to those about her. Sabbath afternoon she became quiet, and passed the time mostly in an unconscious state. At one time she called her nurse to her side, and with a pleasant smile said to her: "So happy, *so happy!*" but was immediately wandering again.

At another time she said, in a lucid moment, "I should love to come back and watch over this seminary. But God will take care of it."

On Monday morning, as a friend entered her room, she greeted her with a sweet smile. On being asked how she did, she replied: "Oh, I am so happy! I am the happiest of the happy. I only wish I could find words to express my happiness."

Monday evening, Mr. Laurie, her pastor, came in to see her. His voice seemed to recall her to consciousness for a little time. He said to her: "Christ precious?" She summoned all her energies to make one great effort, raised both hands, clinched them, lifted her head from her pillow, and exclaimed audibly and with emphasis, "Yes." This was the last word she uttered. Short passages of Scripture were repeated, and her countenance showed that she understood and appreciated them. Those which related to the glory of God seemed to interest her most. She repeatedly made an effort to speak, but without success. Seeing this, Mr. Laurie said to her: "You need not speak; God can be glorified in silence." An indescribable smile came over her countenance in reply, giving her friends very precious assurance that she was leaning on the arm of the Beloved as she passed through the dark valley. An hour after, she had reached the blissful shore, — had joined the company of the redeemed, and been introduced amid the glories which she had so ardently longed to behold.

Thus Mary Lyon was not; for her God had taken her to himself, even as he did Moses, before her eye was dim or her natural force abated. It had not gone so ill with her at Meribah but that she could enter the promised land; and she rests in the inheritance promised her in the holy mount.

The funeral was attended the following Thursday. Rev. Mr. Laurie conducted the services at the seminary. Rev. Dr. Humphrey preached a sermon in the church from the texts: "The path of the just is as the shining light, that shineth more and more unto the perfect day;" "The memory of the just is blessed." Rev. Mr. Harris and Rev. Mr. Swift also took part in the exercises. At the grave, the school sung the hymn commencing, "Sister, thou wast mild and lovely."

Her remains rest in a little enclosure upon the seminary grounds; and the spot is marked by a simple, massive monument of Italian marble.

It had been repeatedly said that if Miss Lyon should be removed, the institution she had founded must change its character; and it did seem, for a time, to those bereaved teachers that they could not go on without her upon whose counsel they had leaned so implicitly. The Lord helped them. If ever his strength was made perfect in weakness, it was during the months that followed March 5th, 1849. The excitement in school was calmed, severe disease was stayed, and the Holy Spirit was with them by his restraining, as well as converting, influences. Though in a few weeks they saw another of their band called suddenly to lay down her armor and enter upon her reward, yet blessings were multiplied unto them. At the end of the year they could only lift up their hearts in thankfulness and praise, in review of the way they had been led.

That summer was a pledge of what the Lord purposed still to do for the institution consecrated to him so entirely and heartily by its founder. Nearly sixteen years have passed since she finished life's conflict; but his hand has ever been over it for good. To-day finds it carrying out the principles upon which it was established, as prosperously as when she left it, and with a larger number of pupils. It is no longer looked upon as an experiment and with suspicion; but it has a name and an important place among the educational institutions of our land. Two seminaries established in Ohio upon similar principles are under the direction of Holyoke graduates, and are very prosperous. The girls' school in Oroomiah is also a daughter of Mount Holyoke. And many of our degraded sisters in that distant land will bless God through all eternity for Mary Lyon, the instructor of their own teachers, Miss Fiske and Miss Rice.

In July, 1862, occurred the twenty-fifth anniversary of the school; and, in commemoration of it, the graduates were all invited to be present. Many of them were able to accept the invitation and join in a glad reunion, in which some of Miss Lyons' friends, who had aided her in her enterprise, united. That was a day of thrilling interest, on which classmates and friends long separated met and reviewed the way in which they had been led, thanked God for the blessings bestowed upon their loved seminary home, and pledged anew their prayerful remembrance of it and of each other.

SELECTIONS

FROM

MISS LYON'S INSTRUCTIONS.

SELECTIONS.

MORNING EXERCISES.

(See page 105.)

I.

"Thy will be done."

We are so constituted that we have strong desires. We would not have it otherwise. But we would have our desires lost in God's will. Parents often speak of a child's possessing a strong will as a very great calamity. It is certainly a calamity to have an unsubdued will, but a blessing to have strong desires yielded to a higher and holier will. The yielding of the will to the parent or teacher is often the schoolmaster that leads to Christ. Thank God if you have learned to submit your will to that of your parents. You have had but little occasion to practise submission now, but I trust you will treasure up this passage of Scripture in your hearts and practise it all your lives. You will often be called to yield your will where you least expected it, and perhaps to those to whom you would not naturally yield it. This is often true in the family relations. Unhappiness in domestic circles might almost always be avoided, if there were only those found to say from the heart, "Not my will, but thine be done."

We may, perhaps, be submissive to the will of God in great events, where we can see his hand, but when his will is made known through the agency of man, find ourselves unsubmissive. This should not be so. His providence makes known his will, and not his audible voice. All that is sent upon you is at his bidding, and he stands ready to help you to know no will but his. We may become like little children, willing to be led just where God would have us go. When we find ourselves ready to give up even lawful pleasures and possessions, how happy is our life! When we can relinquish health and friends and our smile not be disturbed, how much we enjoy them! I think our feelings are somewhat like those of Abraham and Sarah when Isaac was given back to them from Moriah. It is a blessed life to be conscious of doing all we do because God would have it done, and feeling that all we possess is his, and if taken from us will still be found in safe-keeping.

II.

Sowing to the Spirit and to the Flesh.

He who sows to the Spirit and denies himself will have an increase of happiness and great spiritual growth, while those who sow to the flesh, loving self, reap only corruption. The most wretched beings in this world are those who think only of themselves, having no interest in others. How many do we see around us seeking for ease, honor, pleasure, or improvement, just to gratify self. If their object is attained there comes little of happiness with it, because all is expended upon self. We ought to turn the current of feeling toward others. Let it flow out in a thousand streams. How much happier you will be to live in a thousand than to live in yourself alone. The throwing out of your whole soul in powerful, disinterested, vigorous action for others, no matter how self-denying, will make you to receive a hundred-fold even in this life. It is our duty to exhibit to the universe a being enjoying all the happiness for which we were created. How is this to be done? By a forgetfulness of self, and devotion of thought, time, feeling, and money to the interests of others. Thus there will be a constantly-increasing inward realization of real happiness. No one, let him do all he can for others, can make the sacrifice that Christ has made for us. His natural life was as dear to him as any one's, but he gave it all for the good of others. Selfishness contains within itself a canker-worm. Loving self supremely continually disappoints.

Selfishness is our greatest enemy. We may be in danger of following the advice of friends who would lead us to practise less self-denial. I should be afraid to dissuade any one from exercising self-denial. If a sister or a friend is inclined to give up some article of dress, that she may give more to a benevolent object, although she may scarcely meet your ideas of respectability without it, do nothing to change her inclination. If one has or has not a desire to practise self-denial, do nothing which may prevent the exercise of it. The act brings a rich reward, the most blessed recompense that can be asked.

When in doubt which of two courses to take, follow

that which involves most self-denial. You will then find yourself in the safer and happier path, and walking with Him who denied himself for our sakes.

We are told many times in the Bible that we are not to seek our own ease—that our life does not consist in the abundance of the things we possess. We are taught to renounce self. We should first give ourselves to Christ, and then seek, like him, to do good to all about us. He was never seeking a place where to live, but a place where he could deny himself for others.

III.

Study of the Scriptures.

Always have a plan for studying the Scriptures. Make a plan that you will like to follow for years. Seek to give at least two hours of every Sabbath to the careful study of the Scriptures. Read the Bible in course. There is an advantage in this, especially for those who are weighed down with cares, or literary pursuits, or those whose minds are undisciplined. Disinclination to reading is thus overcome. How little we read our Bibles! Might we not find time to read some chapters more every day? Let us think for a moment how we should feel, if a voice from heaven should tell us that we could never open a Bible again.

It is a duty to commit Scripture to memory, and have a plan for self-teaching. Commit passages that interest you, and commit them perfectly. Do not mutilate them. If you have committed them well, when you teach a child, repeat Scripture to a sick person, or pray, it will flow forth easily and be just what is needed.

Bible language is the best body for Bible thoughts. There is a beauty and strength in Scripture language that is found nowhere else. Shakespeare is not worthy of a place by its side. Treasure the words and the truths of the Bible. Make these truths the subject of frequent meditation. We can not depend on the strongest resolutions, or the impulses of immediate feeling; we must be guided by the truth. How much we may accomplish in fifteen years in studying the Bible! It is an inexhaustible mine, and most precious diamonds are found in it, after we think all the gems are dug out. The historical portions reward long-continued and oft-repeated study. We can hardly give too much time to the history of the Israelitish nation. There are three distinct things that we should bear in mind in reference to them. They were the recipients of the oracles of God; through them the Messiah was to come; they were the foundation of the church. More knowledge of human nature is to be derived from the study of the history of the Israelites than from any other source. If we would learn of God, let us read that history. If we would know ourselves, we shall find our hearts well portrayed in it.

When you read the Psalms and the Epistles, dwell carefully on each word, and pray over every verse. Let your soul sometimes delight itself in reading, meditating, and praying at the same time, over your open Bible. The sweet pleasure and satisfaction found in sitting down alone to read the Bible is evidence of being a Christian. How often some verse will come home to the heart as nothing else will! It seems to penetrate deeper than any sermon or religious instruction.

If the Bible may only be allowed to take the lead in our schools, I care not how closely the sciences follow.

IV.

Our relations to God.

Our relations to persons and things around us should keep us constantly alive to duty. We ought to think and reflect upon them, and not go hurriedly from one thing to another, because led by others, but, understanding our relations, with resolution and fixedness of purpose perform our duty. But our relations to God are the most important subjects of study and thought. We should consider them very often, for all our other relations flow from these. It is really the whole great business of life to know and understand our relations to God, and to perform the duties arising from those relations. How great, how comprehensive, is our work! We have a threefold duty—to receive the truth, to believe it, and to obey it. Our minds are so constituted that nothing but God can fill them. He is the only object suitable and capable of satisfying the immortal mind. And the mind craves a spiritual satisfying, almost as the physical system does food. It is the joy of the Christian that God is his Creator, that he lives in Him and receives all good from him. How full are the Psalms of this feeling! The Christian's heaven is being eternally with his God, and in the enjoyment of that bliss of which his communings with him here are only a foretaste. And his thought of hell is only of being banished from the presence of his God for ever and ever.

God is the supreme Governor of the world, and every thing which takes place in it. Every act as it is performed, every thought as it passes through the mind, every word as it is spoken, is incorporated by God into his divine plan of government. Each individual is accountable to God for all he does. We ought to be solemn, knowing that the least thing we do is not overlooked by God. His government extends over the universe; the winds and the waves obey him; the beasts of the fields, the fowls of the air, and the cattle upon a thousand hills; but he has a law for his moral beings. This law is full of glory, and it is easy to be obeyed by a willing heart and an obedient mind. The law of the Lord is perfect. It is so because if changed in the least it would be imperfect. The best laws for nations, communities, schools, or societies are capable of improvement. Not thus with God's law. It is perfect because it treats all alike. He is no respecter of persons. Its commands are in agreement with principles of our nature. It is one of these principles to honor our parents, to love our brothers and sisters. The law of God is easy to be obeyed in health, in sickness, in strength, in weakness, by the wise, the ignorant, the rich, the poor, by all. It is adapted to the wisdom of the wisest, to the poverty of the poorest, to all men in their various conditions. Of what other law can this be affirmed? But no law is perfect without a penalty, otherwise it would be only advice, — and no one but its divine author can judge what it should be. The penalty of God's law is certainly to be inflicted, and rewards for keeping it are equally sure and full of glory.

V.

Willing to Live and Labor.

2 Cor. v. This chapter describes the state of one ready to depart and be with Christ, and yet willing to live and labor. It presents two great principles of action—the terror of the Lord, and the constraining love of Christ. However much we may labor and pray for souls, remember that Christ died for them. We must make effort for the salvation of souls, and that effort must be accompanied by an inward desire and love for the work. There is an internal feeling, which none know but those who have experienced it, that prompts to action, and is never tired of the work, though one may feel that she can not make the mental and physical effort requisite.

If the citadel of the heart is once taken possession of by its rightful sovereign, it can never be retaken by Satan. It may be called the internal heart. Some expect religion to free them from all their infirmities at once. But it will not be so. We groan in this life, being burdened. The evidence that we are renewed is in the effort to counteract every thing that opposes our spirituality. We should not rest because the citadel is taken. We should rather make continued conquests on the outlying provinces. The Christian course requires exertion. It is a race which demands an effort, greater than any physical effort we have ever put forth.

VI.

Cultivation of Personal Religion.

Christians should give much time to cultivating personal religion. This family is not now a standard in this respect. When the daughters of the millennium shall occupy these seats, they will not think a half-hour morning and evening sufficient for devotion. We ought to take care of every hour, making a right division of time, that we may have more for communion with God. To be most careful to meet worldly engagements, and give only the fragments of time to religious duties, is not seeking first the kingdom of God. Our time, as well as our property, should be tithed to the Lord. We should seek to expend it all aright. It is a great thing to know how to rest rightly.

We ought to make progress in religious knowledge. We should daily gain new ideas, or gain a new impression of some idea. We should never hear a sermon or prayer without gaining something. If you will lay your minds and hearts open to the truth, you will find yourselves growing rapidly in religious knowledge, even if your means of grace are not all you would desire. Never feel that you can not get good from ordinary preachers. If you are where God has placed you, He can and will bless you ever and always in his house. Your duty is to hear.

Christians must often go forward in efforts for themselves and others, also, when it seems utterly impossible. Efforts made in such a way cause us to grow rapidly in the strength that God gives. When laboring for souls, we are often called upon to speak the last word we can speak, give the last bread we have, and then look to Christ for more.

We must often pray till we have not another petition that we can offer, and then when in silence we are resting on the Eternal Arm, our friend may be saved.

VII.

"Ye are not your own."

Nothing helps the Christian more in the discharge of his duty, than a sense of his responsibility; but who can duly estimate that responsibility! It increases with every beating pulse. An immortal spirit is committed to him, which is to be an inhabitant of heaven, a companion of Jesus Christ for ever, and there is doubtless a very close connection between our religious character here and our state in the world to come. There is a wonderful adaptation in this world to fitting us for our eternal home. But we may do things here, not only at a wrong time but in a wrong spirit and manner, that will not only affect us all our lives but through eternity. We should look carefully to the manner of performing not only our religious duties, but also our temporal duties, for this also is to affect us through all eternity. Let us remember that time is really a part of eternity. This is our sowing-time, and the reaping is at hand. We are bought with a price; and when we consider what that price was, can we ask to be our own? Would we wish to live for any other than Him who has given his own life for us? What a privilege, what a comfort, that we can all live and labor for Christ!

There are no Christians so young or so weak that they can not labor. All are watchmen. We should all lift up our voice to warn those who see not the sword of God pursuing them. We should all seek to live consistent Christian lives. Perhaps it will be found when the history of every conversion shall be made known, that there has been no louder and more effectual voice than this. God has made it a blessing in every age to be associated with the righteous. Those around you look to you,—they notice you in the room, in the class, in the prayer-meeting, in your calls, your walks, at all times,—in your words, looks, every thing. The consistent life of the young Christian may be a more effectual means for the conversion of youth, than all others combined. You may do much by religious conversation. I do not mean studied conversation, but by always having a heart to speak with Christians before others. Be free to speak of a passage of Scripture that has interested you, of a prayer-meeting, of doing good to souls. The great means of doing good, though we can not tell why or how, only because God so directed it, is by example. We are to be ourselves what we would have others be. And this not only when others know it, but in all places; for I believe that even what we do in secret affects others.

VIII.

Our sinful Hearts.

It is true that we know little of our hearts. If we would know what sin is; if we would know our own character, take the Bible and read every verse, from the beginning, that speaks of sin. Read those passages that describe all. If we appear not as wicked as we are described, it is because of the restraining influences thrown around us. Were those removed our hearts would disclose all this abominable wickedness. Would you see the human heart unsealed, look at the history of the children of Israel. There is a counterpart in our hearts to all that is revealed of them. Would you see God in the silence of your closets, read the history of Israel. We see there his leading attributes, wrath and long-suffering. Dwelling upon these attributes helps us to understand ourselves. The hatred of the human heart towards salvation is greater than towards condemnation. There are delicate young ladies who manifest their contempt for a revival, and if Christ were on earth, they would cry, "crucify him." They would be willing it should be done. This is a hard doctrine to those who know not their hearts. God has shown his displeasure against sin in the penalty, he has annexed, and we shall each know in heaven or hell how great is his displeasure. The sufferings of the Son of God show it most clearly. No language has as yet fully described the wickedness of the human heart. The language of the Bible on this subject is labored. If such is sin, what is its penalty?

IX.

"TAKE NO THOUGHT WHAT YE SHALL EAT."

We think of things of which we ought not to think. We often make ourselves unhappy by dwelling on our condition and prospects, and those of our friends. But it is our blessed privilege to commit all these to him, who will certainly take care of us, if he sees we are not afraid to trust him. What a wonder that the Infinite God is willing to take thought for us, and it is a greater wonder that we are not willing to trust him. With God to take thought for us, we need never be sad. We have only to go on and do present duty, and God will take care of the future. This thought often overwhelms me—God, the great God taking care of me, and willing to let me trust him! If all is dark; if there is universal darkness, and long continued, we may still trust God, if we are willing to obey him. If you are Christ's, do not seek for certainty and security in this life. Jesus never led one of his children in that way. We must trust him.

X.

Eternity.

Eternity is probably more like time than we imagine. All the essential conditions of our existence will, doubtless, continue through eternity; but we shall follow out the shades of condition fully in another world. The difference between slight and excruciating pain is great here, but it will be greater there. Happiness, whether great or little, is important here; but it will be vastly more important there. We are not, perhaps, aware how much of our happiness and misery consists in remembering. There would really be but little enjoyment here were it cut off with the moment and blotted out of our being. How much happiness do we sometimes now enjoy in remembering the past! What will that happiness be in eternity? There we shall remember, with joy, all that was endured to some purpose. The remembrance of wrong living causes us unhappiness here. We have feelings of shame for the moment, but throw a vail over such feelings. It is like looking at the burning sun. We can close the eyelids and shut it out. But, imagine yourself without eyelids. That would be like eternity. There will be no vail there. We forget in this life, but shall remember in eternity. Our remembrances here, compared with those there, will be like the glimmer of a candle before the sun. This life is but a faint picture of eternity. Every thing here is helping to make up our future happiness or misery. In what we think and say we are weaving the web of eternity. The least word here is to live with us through those countless ages. How foolish to yield to temptation, and forget that we are to live for ever. How changed will our views of life be in another world! What views of the Divine character will be revealed to us when we reach the eternal shores.

XI.

"IN THE WORLD YE SHALL HAVE TRIBULATION."

Much has been said, and justly, of the pleasures and enjoyments and blessings given us in this world. Still, it is a life of trial, sorrow, and tribulation. We are oppressed by various ills, and, more than all, by the weight of sin. But there is a remedy for all this. It is looking unto Jesus. And while we can look to him, it is a great mistake to desire to be free from trials. Trials give us our most delightful sympathy with the dear Saviour, and help prepare us to go and dwell with him. Those happy ones who have been washed in the blood of the Lamb, came out of great tribulation. We desire the result, but shrink from the process leading to it. To have sympathy with Christ, we must take up the cross in the path of duty. We need not seek the cross, but we should never try to go around it. It is giving but one view of the Christian life to say it is a life of joy. It is a paradox that the more he suffers the greater will be his joy. There are three kinds of suffering — for sin — the common trials of life — and those trials which we might avoid by going out of the path of duty. The last are those which, if met, give us an exceeding great reward. We should never think of Christ's trial as confined to the last agony. His was a life of constant trials, and we may expect ours to be.

The Saviour kindly remembered our weakness, when he taught us to pray, "lead us not into temptation." We may, and should, ask the Lord every day to lead us where we shall not need to spend our time and strength in resisting temptation, but rather give them directly to his service. We should ask to be free from temptations of pleasure and comfort, no less than those of pain and sorrow. And when tried we should inquire if we have run into the path of temptation.

XII.

The Great Supper.

There yet is room; compel them to come in. We should not pray for the few, who now remain impenitent in this family, because they are left alone. There are many treading the same road with them. Think of the multitudes who die daily on heathen shores. But we should pray for them, because there is yet room in the heart of the Saviour, and because our Father's house is to be filled. Sinners ought to believe that the Redeemer has died for them, and that they may occupy the mansions above. They should compel themselves to come in. Christ has prepared mansions for us, and they will be filled. Does it mean that there are just so many seats in heaven, and that if they are absent there will be a feeling of lack? By no means. Suppose that one of you, for whom prayer has been offered, should not be found in heaven a thousand years hence. Your pious friends there will feel no lack. You will be forgotten. Your name will not come in to disturb the joy of heaven. God will not miss you — your friends will not miss you. Those friends will feel that heaven is filled without you. They will be satisfied with Christ and satisfied with each other.

Each one of you is now called to the supper of the Lamb, and I charge you not to put off repentance for any thing else. You have only a little time in which you may compel yourselves to come in.

AFTERNOON EXERCISES.

(See page 141).

I.

Study.

We should know, by experience, what hard study is. It would be well for all to have one severe study like Latin or mathematics through the year. All should have thorough discipline in these studies before taking the higher English branches. Let the roots grow and expand before we gather fruit. There is no reason why ladies should not faithfully pursue such studies as well as gentlemen. Our course of study embraces much, but probably fifty years hence it will appear quite limited. We should not study to be pleased, any more than we live to eat; and, as it is an important part of discipline not to be fastidious about our food, if we would be prepared for usefulness in any sphere, so we should study and not expect, for a long while, to find pleasure, but when we do reap the fruit it will be very sweet.

At another time she cautioned her pupils against school manners. She said, "You can avoid school tricks, and we do not expect any who come here to practice them. We are a family rather than a school; why have school manners? Never be boisterous; treat all with respect. Let the Bible have its full influence upon your hearts, and you will be gentle, and at the same time happy. I am always afraid of those who talk a great deal about what they are doing. Some of the most efficient characters in the world are the most quiet. Cultivate the habit of moving noiselessly, so that you will always be welcome in the chamber of sickness and suffering.

Benevolence is drawn out in the house-keeping department. In arranging the work we look at justice, while you should look at the other side. It is important for you to be very quiet in the domestic hall. In the rattling of crockery, knives, and forks, and other articles, character is read, and your own mothers honored or dishonored.

II.

Punctuality.

Perfect punctuality in the time and manner of doing things is of great consequence. Consider well what you can and ought to do, and be faithful in performing it. If you form the habit of being a minute or two late it will grow upon you, and you will become very uncomfortable members of society. You will find yourselves neglected, losing your influence, becoming very unhappy, and, may be, doubting even whether you are Christians, just from the effects of the habit of being a little behind time." She here drew a picture of a family wanting in system and punctuality — their hurry and confusion; their chasing of the hours, never to find them, were vividly portrayed. We should be careful, be prompt in paying little debts. It might be impossible, when praying for some one, to keep out of mind a ten cents her due.

Always be within a half a minute of the time appointed for any exercise or duty. Carry this through life, and always let your influence be felt for good in punctuality in attending meeting. Our own punctuality will greatly assist us in the care of others.

III.

Habits.

Every confirmed habit of doing little things well will have an influence upon our future. Our wardrobes should always be kept in order, because of the effect such a habit will have upon ourselves and others. Good habits will enable mothers to have greater moral power over their daughters, and daughters should come up to their mothers' standard in every thing, thus inciting the mothers to higher and higher endeavors, so that each generation will increase in moral perfection, till the dawn of the millennium. We give others much vexation and trouble by negligence. We should form a strong resolution to avoid, through life, trying the patience or irritating the feelings of others in this manner, and strive to possess those habits which will make us welcome visitors any where, and valuable friends.

Oh! if I were as young as you, with my present views, how differently would I begin. Not that I really desire to be put back where you are, for I can say, "Goodness and mercy have followed me all the days of my life;" but I do wish you to begin right. I entreat you to form good habits. You have no time or strength to spare in overcoming bad habits.

Although we are generally neat in the arrangement of the house, we need not expect in this, or any thing else, to find our duty less because by habit we acquire the power of doing it readily, for in just such proportion shall we always find our duties increase. Our amount of duty will always be equal to our amount of strength or ability to perform it. We should be perfect in all we do, not merely for the present, but to help in the formation of a good character. We should not be like soapstone, that crumbles as it is rubbed, but like gold, that shines brighter and brighter the more it is used.

IV.

ECONOMY.

Economy consists in providing well at little comparative expense. It implies good judgment and good taste. It can be equally manifested in the tasteful decorations of a palace and in the simple comforts of a cottage. If all ladies possessed it in a high degree, how much more would be found, in families, of comfort and convenience; of taste and refinement; of education and improvement; of charity and good works. Our institution is distinguished by its economical features. Economy, however, is not adopted for its own sake principally, but as a means of education; as a mode of producing favorable effects upon character, and of preparing young ladies for the duties of life. The great object is to make the school really better. An economical character is to be formed by precept, by practice, and by example. Example has great effect, not only in furnishing a model for imitation, but also in proving that economy is practicable, which is one of the most essential requisites for success. Let a young lady spend two or three years on intimate terms in a family distinguished for a judicious and constant illustration of this principle, and the effect can not be lost. Economy should be strict, and based on principle. It should extend to the smallest things. Those who resolve upon economy on some sudden occasion, or from some unusual motive, are apt to misplace it and appear mean. For instance, a lady may, in listening to some appeal for benevolence, resolve to be very economical, and, when her house is filled with guests, have it but partially lighted. She will be considered mean, and it would not be strange if, after six months, she should go to the opposite extreme. But if she has a fixed habit of economy, her house will be well lighted when it is necessary, and those same lights will be extinguished when there is no further need of them. Proper economy will be an unostentatious habit, offensive to to no one, because regulated by wisdom from above, and will greatly promote the cause of Christ. In practicing it, we shall influence hundreds, and they, in their turn, thousands. We can not expect the blessing of God if we waste what he gives us.

We should economize in nothing more than in time, and be very careful of the time of others. Young ladies are in great danger of using the time of others too freely, and perhaps never more in danger than on recreation day.

V.

Health.

I know it will be a great self-denial to many of you not to study in recreation hours, but we think we have assigned as many hours in a day to study as are advisable. If you can not see things just as we do, we hope you will be willing to yield your judgment to ours. If you have brought good health with you, we think our arrangements are such that, with the blessing of God, you will be enabled to keep it. I would say to you what I have said to many young ladies: the value of health is inestimable to a lady. Her appropriate duties are so numerous and varied, so constant in their demands, and so imperious in the moment of their calls, that health is to her above price. She can not perform her duties faithfully and successfully unless she possesses a calm mind, an even temper, a cheerful heart, and a happy face. To possess all these, will require a good degree of health. A gentleman may possibly do good without much health, but what can a lady do, unless she takes the attitude of an invalid, and seeks to honor Christ by patience and submission. I would not undervalue this, but if you can do good in another way, by taking care of your health, will you not be happier in it? If a gentleman can not do his work one hour, perhaps he may do it another; but a lady's duties admit of no compromise of hours.

If a gentleman is annoyed and vexed with the nervousness of his feeble frame, he may perhaps use it to some advantage, as he attempts to move the world by his pen. But a lady can not make use of this infirmity in her influence over her children and family; an influence which should, at all times, be under the control of gentleness and equanimity. I am very anxious in regard to your health and comfort. If you are Christ's now, or if you become his, remember that he has redeemed your bodies as well as your souls. He is to present them pure and spotless before your Father in heaven. These bodies are not your own. They are the temple of the Holy Ghost. Can you be negligent of them? We will try to help you take care of them. If we think that you should see a physician at any time, we hope you will be willing to do it, — that you will avoid unnecessary exposure, — and seek for a quiet, happy frame of mind, which greatly promotes good health.

God has instituted laws for the regulation of health, and the difference between the moral law and the natural and physical law is, that the former is right in itself, and can never be set aside; and the latter derive their authority from God's appointment: but he has given us a certain degree of elasticity, which makes it safe for us to turn aside when duty requires it. We ought never to lessen this elasticity by using it for self-indulgence. Illustrated by the difference between a mother's depriving herself of her accustomed sleep to care for her sick infant, and doing the same for self-gratification.

Remember, the command, "Thou shalt not kill," means not only outright, but slowly; it means not only others but yourself, not only this generation but generations to come. It is probable that many of you are now suffering from the fact that those who have gone before you have not properly cared for their health. Your mothers, when at your age, were not living for themselves alone — they lived for you, even as they have done in later years. It is a fearful thing, young ladies, to disregard the laws of health. You know not where the consequences may cease. This view of the subject makes life more noble and important. I should not dare to speak to those of little cultivation of mind and heart as I do to you; but I expect *you* to appreciate what I say, and to weigh the subject carefully before God.

VI.

Furnishing a Table.

There are three ways of furnishing a table — the luxurious, the scanty, and the comfortable. The first we often find among the fashionable — but not among the most intellectual. It causes depression of both mind and body. The second, the scanty, causes more depression still. Those who practice the third think very little about their food. Eating is not their great object. It is desirable to give attention to our tables as well as to our souls. I consider bread-making of so much consequence, that, in giving attention to it, I am confident that I am serving God.

PERSONAL RESPONSIBILITY IN GIVING.

(See page 175).

It is nothing with God to help, whether with many, or with them that have no power. But his blessing is delayed so as to be given, as a rich reward, to the willing and obedient heart. Is the spirit of any one stirred within him in behalf of this cause, let him be faithful in his own place and in his own way, and for himself alone. Let him carry his own petition, warm from his own heart, to the throne of mercy, rather than to seek a friend to carry it in his behalf, and it shall prevail. Let him give all — all that he ought, either from his abundance or from his scanty store, rather than to look to his neighbor to do it in his stead, and the deed shall be remembered in heaven, and his work shall not be in vain. Is he poor, let him be careful to give the last mite which the Lord requires at his hand. That little pittance which he has laid aside, which he really seems to need for his comfort, and on which his eye is now fixed with that anxious inquiry, may be more in the Lord's treasury than thousands in other hands. It may be of more weight in the counsels of heaven, as this great question relative to the funds of the American Board shall there be settled.

Is he rich, let him give — not a part — but all which the Lord requires. Though he may cast his thousands into the treasury of the Lord, it may weigh naught in the counsels of heaven if any thing is kept back. But let him come fully up to his ability; let him come fully up to the urgency of the case, and he shall receive even a richer reward than did the widow with her two mites. No one knows to whom in this case it shall be said, "Thou hast power with God and hast prevailed." No one knows to whom the balancing may be given, which shall determine this great question in the court of heaven. The balancing power was given to Achan, and, with his wedge of gold, he could trouble the whole camp of Israel. The deciding power was given to Phineas, and, with javelin in hand, he was able, by a single act, to stay the plague, and save thousands from a speedy death. Let no one say, therefore, that the little which he can do will have no avail. When God, in the court of heaven, shall weigh the offerings which shall decide this great question, he may say, "This poor widow hath cast in more than they all." On the other hand, let no one feel that he can afford to consume treasures on himself, because he has already done so much for the cause. The little that remains in his hand which he can give, and which the Lord requires of him, may be the balancing power which shall decide the whole case. But let each, in his own condition, be faithful unto the last mite, and he shall have his reward. With his faithful hands and willing heart, and through that grace by which he is what he is, let him go, in the name of Jesus, and carry his petition to the mercy seat, and it shall be granted. Is his petition that the hearts of others shall be opened to go and do likewise? Then the hearts of others shall be opened, and they shall go and do likewise, and the work shall be done.

BENEVOLENCE.

March 30, 1848. The duty of sacred charity is plainly inculcated in the Scriptures. The highest form of this charity is that which goes out of ourselves, which is not concerned with ourselves or our interests. Other charities may partake of the true spirit of giving — while other motives are involved. If this great principle is paramount other charities will flow out of it, illustrated by a church, by individuals. The church that will give for the conversion of the world, will give for the salvation of her country. A church needs a foreign mission to teach it to carry its prayers and efforts out of itself; so the man who will give to send the gospel to the heathen, will educate his son to promote the same cause. Pray over this subject while you are considering it; remember it morning and evening. I trust we shall all have our hearts drawn out together, each class of us, that we who hope we are Christians, may take a higher stand, and that we may, in connection with this, first give ourselves to the Lord.

March 31. Sacred charity is a divine appointment, wonderful though it is. The design of this is evidently the benefit of the giver as well as the receiver. Sacred charity is a pledge of personal consecration; a test to one's self of willingness to give up all for Christ. In order that it may be thus, it must be a *heart* work; there must be a readiness to give up all, if God requires it. In the heart all must be given up, and all may enjoy the privilege. Let us all enjoy it.

April 4. Sacred charity is a pledge of personal consecration. It may be made the *test;* if we give up in heart, we shall have an opportunity to carry it out in our lives. The disciple is not above his master — illustrated in the lives of the apostles. Trials for Christ's sake were different in different ages. We may not suffer persecution, but we may give so much as to suffer in the opinion of others; of those, too, whom we love, and the trials be the same in essence as of those who suffer persecution: and we shall not lose the reward. If we give in sacred charity, and give for Christ's sake, we must give so as to feel the loss of what we give continually. I dare not tell any one how much to give; but I have no doubt of certain great principles of which this is one, that we ought voluntarily to submit to suffer in person and in feeling for Christ's sake. Do you feel willing to make such a surrender of all as to give in charity just as much as you believe duty, without conferring with flesh and blood, your own wants, and the wants of those you tenderly love?

April 7. Christian charity may be so practiced and illustrated as to make us feel what a price was paid for our redemption. When you put your hand to this work — always remember, "We are bought with a price." Christ's example should be a motive to us. "For ye know the grace of our Lord Jesus Christ, how that for our sakes he became poor." Shall we be willing to make no return? Oh, I would have our offering made with such a spirit that it shall be the means of setting before us Jesus Christ and him crucified.

April 11. We are to study God's plan, and not

man's. This is a large plan. There are reasons for giving while connected with this seminary, and giving here, this year, rather than at home: reasons, also, for giving only to two *great* objects; these embrace the others. We should remember the principle on which this institution was founded, and the way in which the money was raised for it. It was not to save the money of parents or of children that so much was given here with so little expense to the scholars, but that great and important principles might be inculcated here.

April 13. No plan but God's plan should be adopted. This is large, and should be so large as to have a chastening influence upon us. We may bear some of the same fruits with Christ. We are to give our money to save souls. If we here, this year, give and pray as we should, we shall meet souls, at last, saved through our instrumentality. Great giving meets the will of God. The standard of Christians is too low. I *censure no one*, but I must tell you what I think, that the standard of most of our good people is *too low*. We may give too much for the poor, though I do not think we do. But there is no danger of giving too much for the salvation of *souls*, and we must give now — not wait till we get rich. The telegraphic wires are established between us and the heathen; and if we do not work now, do not send them the gospel now, they will perish. Illustrated by the great Jewish economy. The terms of the gospel itself should lead us to give largely; the terms of discipleship, as given by Christ, also. We must deny ourselves; forsake all that we have. This may be done by changing our style of dress and of living. I do not think the standard I have been presenting is too high. When, in eternity, I meet you and the many others I have here addressed, I think you will all agree with me. And now you ask what you shall do. I can not tell you. I can only spread a few of my many thoughts before you. I can not unburden my soul as I would. Seek wisdom from on high.

April 14. Miss Lyon gave her reasons for having two subscriptions annually, instead of one; alluded to ways in which we may save money intrusted to us by our parents to give away, and then left it with us and our God, praying that all might be blessed.

June 27. This morning Miss Lyon dwelt upon the truth, "God is love" — especially upon that love which was manifested in giving up the *Son* of his love for those who were his enemies. She invited us to try to *think* of this theme, though it is beyond thought to know it — it *passeth* knowledge. As we were about to renew our missionary subscription, the subject was applied to *giving;* she hoped that our second subscription would not be a mere gathering of the fragments, but that many would give so much as to *feel it;* and, more than this, that some would, first of all, give *themselves* unto the Lord, and then never count any sacrifice too great for Christ. She urged all to bear in mind that she was not speaking for the present merely, but she would fain give impressions which will live after she dies, and asked that, when we should hear of her death, we would remember what she had told us this morning of the love of Christ.

July 6. Self-denial, illustrated in the life of a foreign missionary, "How often do I wish that once again I could see all my dear missionary children together for one hour — and what would I say to them? I would not commend them for what they had done. I would sympathize deeply with them in every trial they should speak of; but I should want to spend more of the hour in pointing out the temptations I should fear for them; in telling them how they might fail to be *true missionaries*." Then, for the sake of those present, who might some time find themselves in a heathen land, she pointed out some of the dangers, such as the desire to improve their style of living, so as not to fall so far below the foreign residents with whom they might have intercourse, or a wish to approach more nearly to the style of the native aristocracy, in order, as it might seem, to get an influence over them. Their purse, she said, would be very small, like a child's purse, and yet they might have temptations to make a wrong use of that little. She would not care to have our missionaries receive more for their support, lest they would be less useful, though she would like to have them receive more *to do good* with, if they had the opportunity. In their outfit, and in all their course, she would have them study to see how *little* they might expend on *themselves*. This she ventured to say to *us*, though she would not say it to the *world;* just as she would whisper in the ears of her children who had become *pastors' wives*, to be satisfied with a very small salary, though she would not say the same to their *parishioners*. Then she charged us to remember that she would not take off the burden from those that remain by the stuff, and put it on those " who go out to battle," for she was sure she did not love those less than those at home; but she thought she could not have shown us better what should be *our standard* for self-denial than in thus speaking of missionaries, which very name, she thought, synonymous with self-denial.

OUTLINES OF ADDRESSES ON MISSIONARY CONTRIBUTIONS.

I.

General Principles of Giving.

1. We are not our own, in the use of temporal things.

2. We are to live for eternity in the use of money. This is possible. Many think it is not. Fix your eye on eternity just as it is. Every dollar you spend, cast your eye into eternity.

3. The will of God is to be our only guide. God has a mind on the subject; he has a will. Are you willing to know his mind and will?

4. The will of God can be known. Whoever seeks with his whole heart, shall know it. Three ways — 1. The Word — this must be first. 2. The providence of God. 3. The Spirit of God.

5. The general principle of following the calls of Providence, in doing good, rather than our feelings of ability, is to be applied to this duty.

6. To give as much as we think we ought, is an easy duty.

7. An important test of Christian character.

II.

The Reward.

1. The reward comes to all. No respecter of persons. 2 Cor. viii. 12. The gospel tolerates no compromise of principle with the world. Christ must have all or none. Whoever will give a cup of cold water, will lay down his life.

2. There is a direct reward of Providence. "Hundred-fold."

3. Reward in our own bosoms: —

(*a*) Peace of conscience.

(*b*) A supply for the natural cravings of our nature.

(*c*) Satisfaction in doing what God requires.

(*d*) A feeling of union with Jesus Christ, in his work and his sympathies.

4. Meeting with the fruits of our labor.

5. A personal interest in the greatest events and greatest deeds.

6. The glorious future reward, which is a continuance of the hundred-fold in this life.

III.

Giving in Christ's Name.

1. To give in Christ's name, we must give as much as he requires. He will allow of no compromise. Ananias and Sapphira.

2. We must give with a feeling of our unworthiness. Those who make the greatest sacrifices, have the most feeling of their unworthiness to do it.

3. We must feel that we have a privilege in this world given us through the blood of Christ.

4. We must have just views of Christ's poverty. No merit to be poor — none to be rich. But to be poor as Christ was is accepted.

5. Submissive to Christ's will. Command of Christ. Matt. x. 8–10; John xxi. 15–19.

6. With feelings for others similar to Christ's.

7. With such a view of the reward as Christ had. Heb. xii. 2; xi. 24–27.

IV.

The Bible Standard of giving, high.

1. The general tenor of the Bible gives this impression: Let any candid reader, without prejudice, receive the Bible impression. Darkness and blindness of selfishness on this subject. This darkness does not cease with the selfish mind, but extends to darken the views of the benevolent.

2. Evidence of a high standard from the Jewish economy. The requirements of God uniform in principle, not uniform in the detailed application. Time, money, fruits of the earth, to be given in how many ways. Riches discouraged; year of jubilee; non-intercourse with foreign nations. The great principle of discouraging riches, not to be applied in detail.

3. Early disciples required to give up all, and become poor, for Christ's sake. Houses and lands to be forsaken. The principle continued. All suffer tribulation not in the same way, but in some way. All poorer than they would be. A false impression is sometimes

made by saying that no one was ever poorer for what he gives.

4. Early community of goods. Acts iv. 34–37.
5. The curse for withholding. Acts v.; Mal. iii.
6. The blessings promised to the liberal.
7. Commendation of extraordinary giving. Luke xxi. 1–4; 2 Cor. viii. 1–4.
8. The example of Christ as held up to us. 2 Cor. viii. 9.

V.

Reasons why we should adopt the Bible Standard.

1. The value of the soul. Dwell on it, and compare it with the uses of money. Matt. xvi. 26.
2. The infinite price paid for its redemption.
3. The duty of loving others as ourselves. Apply this to their future state.
4. The divine appointment of means.
5. Doors opened by the providence of God.
6. Success that God has given to the use of means.
7. The great cloud of witnesses.
8. Our knowledge of duty — of what can be done.
9. The demands of our own consciences.

VI.

What is a high Standard?

In such a great work, reason would often seem to require that we give up all. But if we can find a general guide in the Bible, we may, from it, take permission to keep a part for ourselves.

Tenth. The generally admitted proportion, if any,

taken from the Jewish tribes. Two great mistakes in this standard.

1. About the Jewish tribe. A tenth a small part of what was required.

2. In what, in our circumstances, would be a tenth. Some take a tenth of their income after supporting their families. Others take a tenth after their own personal support. Others still calculate to take their salary exclusive of board, not reckoning their board any thing. Some take only the money from produce sold, leaving out the produce consumed, — the house-rent, the use of horse and carriage, etc.

The Jewish standard a general guide, but not a correct one for individual duty.

The Old Testament our school-master to teach us New Testament duty. All such requirements allow of some deviations. The disciples might pluck the ears of corn on the Sabbath. But deviations must be higher as well as lower.

Two grounds of deviation. First ground, our ability compared with that of the Jews. The following points of comparison: —

1. Our country, with Palestine. The land to cultivate, how much more. The arts, which increase the value of property. The knowledge, enabling us to use what we have to the best advantage.

2. Compare the immediate community in which you live with the whole country.

3. Compare your own standing with all the others.

Second ground of deviation. Comparison between the two dispensations: —

1. The object of the sacrifice required. Ceremonial burdens removed, but in their stead the command, "Go ye into all the world."

2. The great High Priest. Heb. viii. 1–6; ix. 8–14. The Jewish priests to be sustained in their work. If I may be allowed the expression, the Great High Priest needs far more to sustain his work. His sacrifice greater.

3. The direct requirements of Christ to forsake all. The young man. Matt. xix. 21. Not so explicit in the case of the Old Testament saints.

4. The voluntary sacrifice of the early Christians to extend the gospel. Not so with the Old Testament saints.

5. The new covenant compared with the old. What encouragement to work for God under this new covenant, with such promises. Heb. viii. 7–12.

General conclusion, that the standard which God has raised far higher than that of the most liberal.

VII.

Self-denial for Christ's sake.

2 Pet. ii. 20–24; Heb. ii. 10–18.

1. What is self-denial? Not what is brought on by Providence, but by your voluntary act.

2. Christ designs sufferings for his disciples. No other dare to enter into the sheepfold only to follow Christ.

3. Self-denial is painful for the time. It was with Christ. It was a bitter cup. So with his followers.

Giving your money as you ought will be a painful work. Whoever doubts it, look at the excuses made against it.

4. It is the most painful of suffering. The struggle of yielding to the stroke more painful than the stroke itself.

5. It is crowned with an unspeakable joy. Not a joy beforehand but afterwards. Christ has this joy; this hope to sustain us. Christ was thus sustained.

6. The Captain of our salvation "perfect through suffering."

(1.) Captain in seeking an atonement for us.

(2.) In sanctifying us.

(3.) In leading us on in the conflict of self-denial.

(4.) In giving us final victory.

7. He calls us brethren.

8. We are to look to Christ in his sufferings.

9. We are to behold him as the Son of God there, and when we come back from the sight shall we say I can not do this, or bear this, or suffer this?

10. We are to look to him as ever able to redeem us.

VIII.

Reasons for Self-denial.

John xii. 25–30.

1. A reward is given our labors: —

(1.) Success direct.

(2.) Success in prospect.

(3.) Success with others to carry it on.

2. Religious communications in your own soul.

(1.) Reality of the unseen world. That of misery and of blessedness.

(2.) Communion with Christ — his world — his object — his plans — his promises.

(3.) Faith in the grand doctrine of salvation. We are to work on the same principle that Christ did. Not that they love us, but that we love them.

(4.) Daily dependence on Christ — his promises — his grace.

(5.) An advancing onward in our pathway to heaven. How is one to get out from the influence of the world?

3. Our final reward: —

(1.) Being with Christ.

(2.) Sharing in his glory.

(3.) Our joy and causes of rejoicing.

(4.) Rejoicing with Christ.

IX.

Curse of Selfishness.

Mal. i. 6, 7, 8, 14; iii.

What is it to rob God? Not to give what he requires. All the tithes. Learn this from, —

(1.) Jewish dispensation.

(2.) Christian precepts.

(3.) Christ's example.

1. Curse on your person.
2. Curse on your relative business with others.
3. Curse on the work of your hands.
4. Curse on all the blighted feelings of your heart.

5. Curse in having no heart for the work of self-denial — the talent laid up in the napkin.

X.

The Parable of the Talents.

Matt. xxv. 14–30.

Great variety of instruction in this parable. It is the plan of God that all should *live on little.*

1. God has given on an average but little to the human family. Each, of course, must take but little and use it.

2. By the great law of love, God demands of each much of the little he has given him. This principle essential to meet this demand.

3. By the duty to co-operate with Christ God has made a special demand on the little. This principle essential to meet this demand.

4. God has opened a wide door into the field of his service, and thus made a demand on the little.

5. The increasing calls of Providence more than keep pace with all other increasing improvements.

Look at the improvements in property by agriculture — the arts — railroads — manufactures — commerce, etc.; and then look at China, at India, at Persia, at Africa, at the Islands of the Sea.

6. It is the only way to be a consistent Christian. Without this established principle of action there will be inconsistencies and absurdities.

7. The only way to be relieved from perplexing embarrassment with regard to duty.

8. The only way to receive continued peace of conscience; and

9. The glorious reward in heaven.

Apply this to yourselves; educate yourselves by doing. Do not excuse yourselves.

1. Either because you are so rich or so poor. Peculiar advantages of each.

2. Defer not to the future what is to be done now.

3. Do not forget.

4. Never faint nor be discouraged.

5. Keep eternity and the worth of the soul in view.

6. Keep your eye on the Saviour, day by day, in this work.

MEETINGS WITH THE IMPENITENT.

(See page 107).

1848. *Jan.* 3, Fast-day. Miss Lyon met all those in the Seminary hall who usually meet with her on the Sabbath. After singing and prayer, she commenced by inviting those who could answer the following questions affirmatively, to meet with her at seven o'clock this evening: Does it seem to you that you want religion? Do you feel that *now* is the time to seek it? Does it seem to you that you are willing to give up the world? Does it seem to you that you are willing to attend to it, even though ridiculed for it by your best friends, even if you knew you must be alone in seeking it? Does it seem to you that you want your will bowed to God's? Do you want all your portion in God? Do you want to be entirely employed in the service of God? Do you want that religion that shall make you to care for souls?—Upon each of these questions she dwelt. All who could answer them in the affirmative, were to write a note saying they would like to attend the meeting. She then went on to speak to the other class, who could not thus decide, mentioned the various excuses made by sinners for not *now* seeking salvation, and submitting to Jesus; and showed how vain they were; how vain they would seem in the light of eternity. Her closing remark was, "How vain to resist God! Did you ever see the little insect fall into the flame; see it struggle and strive to escape? — how vain! Just so you are in the hands of an *angry* God. What if you do resist? What are *you*, a feeble worm of the dust? Oh, how vain! how much better to submit!"

Nearly sixty attended the meeting in the evening. The Christians met at the same hour in praying circles.

Jan. 10. The meeting, at four, was one of great solemnity. Before commencing her remarks, Miss Lyon invited to a meeting, at seven, all those who felt pained at the thought that this work might cease, and they be passed by. Her subject was, Christ Jesus and him crucified. About forty wrote notes to attend the meeting in the evening. At the same hour a meeting was appointed for all those who had some hope that they had this year found the Saviour. There were thirty-eight present. It seems as though God was trying his children, to see how faithfully they will labor and pray. Last year the Spirit was literally poured out; we could only stand still and say, "What hath

God wrought!" Now he blesses, just as the means are used.

Jan. 12, Recreation-day. Religious meetings this P. M., as last week. Those who meet with Miss Lyon on the Sabbath, were invited to do so to-day. Most were there. Sectional prayer-meetings, also, as last week.

Jan. 16, Sabbath. At the meeting in the P. M. Miss Lyon spoke from the words, "Choose ye this day whom ye will serve," and, "To-day if ye will hear his voice." At the close, she invited all who had decided to-day, that they would serve the Lord, and those who had to-day felt an uncommon anxiety to decide thus, —to a meeting in her room. There were seventeen present (there had been forty-seven present at a meeting in the morning, for all who have indulged hope recently); Miss Lyon is rather worn; her anxiety for the family, and what she should say as she has met us from time to time, has been very great of late.

Feb. 7. A meeting was appointed yesterday (Sabbath), the first Sabbath after vacation, for those who have indulged a hope this year. If any one who attended a meeting of the same kind before vacation, felt that she ought not to do so now, she was to write a note; or, if any who had not attended had some hope now, they too were to write a note. Five new ones attended. One was not there who had been before. She wrote no note, however.

Feb. 13, Sabbath. Of the large class who were without hope, at the beginning of last term, more than half now trust they have found the Saviour. In the meeting this P. M. Miss Lyon read, "I thank thee that thou hast hid these things from the wise and prudent," etc. And then spoke of the display of Sovereign grace in the salvation of sinners; of the pardon of the sinner; of important periods in the life of every sinner; when the kingdom comes near; of the danger of passing those periods; there must be a last one. Be entreated to be reconciled to God, to believe on the Lord Jesus Christ. Those who hope you have done so, do it anew, do it continually; those who have never done it, do it to-day.

Feb. 27, Sabbath. Object of these meetings, to aid them in seeking religion. If they have failed in this they are all in vain. She said a burden rested on her soul every Sabbath, as she looked forward to this meeting. She read the account of the publican, and spoke of the way in which religion must be sought; first, there must be a determination to seek it, in spite of all that may be said and done by others. It must be sought with a sense of our own unworthiness; with a willingness to venture all, to run the risk of failing or succeeding.

March 5, Sabbath. Miss Lyon invited to her room, in the morning, all who had a general interest; who felt that they wanted, more than any thing else, to seek the salvation of their souls. There were as many present as could sit round the room.

March 19. The duty and importance of "considering." Miss Lyon then invited to a meeting in her room, at seven, all who were ready to decide to consider the question, this week, of being Christians, whatever others might do. Ten were present.

April 9. Miss Lyon's subject was the "New Song"

spoken of in Revelation. It was addressed more particularly to those who hope they have already learned a little of that "Song." At the close of the meeting she invited to her room, at seven, all those who thought that the Holy Spirit was still striving with them. She mentioned some things that would help them to judge whether he was; as she wished them to decide, remembering God's eye was upon them, and be careful that they did not grieve him away entirely by deciding to stay away. Seventeen came (all but sixteen who are without hope).

April 23, Subject, "*To-day.*" This, the last of these meetings for this term. Alluded to the past and the future; once more entreated those who are yet without hope, to come and make their peace with God. At the close of the meeting, she invited to a meeting all those who were not interested, and yet wished to be, and would be willing that others should know that they were interested.

OUTLINES OF SABBATH-EVENING INSTRUCTIONS.

I.

WHO ARE AT THE ELEVENTH HOUR.

Matt. xx. 1–16.

All acknowledge that the aged are. But the young may be.

1. Those appointed to an early death.
2. Those who have enjoyed, but have misimproved many privileges.

3. Those who have often grieved the Spirit.

4. Those who are enjoying their last special call.

Who believe yourselves at the eleventh hour? Urgent reasons why those of you at the eleventh hour should enter the vineyard.

1. The infinite importance that you should be saved. What can be the gain if your soul is lost?

2. The voice of encouragement from the Saviour.

3. The calls of the Spirit to your heart. Who are now thus called?

4. Christ has need of your feeble services.

5. By your salvation can be magnified the riches of grace.

II.

God our Portion.

Receiving God as the portion of the soul, often the first exercise of the renewed heart.

Let us dwell on this portion. During these communings, may some one receive God as her portion.

1. God, and only God, can fill the soul with satisfying delight.

2. There is a great, solemn, and real delight in feeling that God is incomprehensible. The wicked seek to comprehend God, and deny what they can not comprehend.

3. All difficulties and perplexities can be referred to God, and there left.

4. The feeling, "God will do right."

5. There is an awful and solemn delight in the feeling that God hates sin. When we struggle against sin, it is comforting to know that there is One who hates and abhors all sin as it deserves.

6. God knows our unworthiness, guilt, dependence, and want.

7. God can forgive sin.

8. Christ, the only door by which we can be admitted to the presence of God.

9. The great end of Christ's sufferings and death to reconcile us to God, restore us back to his favor and presence. 2 Cor. v. 17–21.

Thus sinners may be entreated to be reconciled to God.

III.

Enemies of Christ.

What is it *now*, to be the enemies of Christ? What will it be at the judgment day, and what in eternity?

1. There are enemies. Are you his enemies?

2. They forget Christ. They do not feel his presence.

3. They do not feel his excellence and glory.

4. They are not affected with his history — his life and death.

5. The cross is to them foolishness. Here is an exhibition of sin; of the mind of a sinner; of pardon; of. deliverance; of the Godhead, and all his glory, — his wisdom, his justice, his mercy, his power, his glory; but they see it not.

6. They despise the cross, and Jesus, who died on the cross.

What will it be, at the judgment, to be Christ's enemy?

1. Christ will come.

2. This will fill his enemies with terrible anguish. The face of the Lamb. This, more than any other view of God in Christ. Why?

(1.) He is the sinner's friend, but their eternal enemy.

(2.) Their friend once, but now their enemy.

(3.) His countenance once beamed with infinite compassion; now, with a heart-rending fervor.

(4.) Once, his voice they heard in accents of invitation; now, of eternal banishment.

What will it be to be his enemy in eternity?

The exciting, the changing, the passing scenes even of the terrible judgment will be some relief; but oh, the dark, the changeless, the eternal prison of despair! Banishment for ever from Jesus Christ. Never to see his face, or hear his voice, or one of his friends, or one of his works. But remember him as once your friend, but now your eternal enemy.

IV.

Friends of Christ.

Rev. v. 9–12; vii. 9–17.

Are any of you his friends? Have you a faint impression that it may be so? Most of you know you are his enemies. Would you become his friends to-day?

1. Present state of his friends. They have the feelings and conduct of friends.

(1.) They regard and love his character. What a combination in Christ!

(2.) They feel that they have sinned against a friend. Peter and Judas.

(3.) They have confidence in him as a friend.

(4.) They are grateful to him as to a friend.

(5.) They seek to honor him as a friend.

(6.) They delight in having his will done. What is the prominent manifestation of his will? To save sinners.

(7.) They do his will.

2. Condition of his friends at the judgment day.

(1.) His glorious appearance.

(2.) The sweetness of his voice.

(3.) His protection from Divine wrath, as every idle thought and every deed is brought into judgment.

(4.) The blessed find sentence.

3. Condition of his friends in eternity.

(1.) For ever with the Lord.

(2.) Never sin again. Never do a wrong or careless deed again.

(3.) No sickness nor sorrow.

(4.) Never see any one sin again.

5. No end to the increasing joy. How shall any one become Christ's friend?

(1.) It is described as believing.

(2.) As a reunion.

(3.) As a receiving. All invited.

What God does in this great work is unknown to us. It will be our adoration through eternity whether we know or not. What we do is very simple. We fail because it is so little more than because it is so much. "Go work."

5. Every one is now invited to become his friend.

6. The dreadful guilt and misery of those who refused to become Christ's friend.

V.

Meeting at the Judgment.

After death knowledge of many things, and experience not had here. But the realities of the judgment not all human. Long suspense

(1.) Of the wicked. Fearful forebodings. Dreadful suspense it may be.

(2.) Of the righteous. Confidence in Christ satisfies the mind.

The judgment will come. What a great and *long* meeting. Who will there meet who have long been separated? Such vivid recollections, who could bear? Those who lean on the arm of Christ can bear the same.

1. Cain and Abel.
2. Noah and the men who reviled him.
3. Abraham and those whom he left in Ur of the Chaldees.
4. Esau and Jacob.
5. Lot and the men of Sodom.
6. Pharaoh and Moses.

7. David and Saul.

8. David and his son Absalom.

9. Ahab and Elijah.

10. Hezekiah and his father Ahaz.

11. Josiah and his father Amon.

12. Jeremiah and those whom he warned and entreated.

13. Stephen and his persecutors.

14. Paul and his persecutors.

15. Peter and Judas.

Whom will you meet?

Your father; your mother; your teachers; your brothers; your sisters; your minister, — all whom you knew on earth who love Christ. Where will you be? Where will you go?

VI.

SINNERS SPENDING WITH RIOTOUS LIVING.

Luke xv. Describe the young man.

1. Goods spent. Thoughts; conversation; heart; time; intellectual powers; social powers; Sabbaths; seasons for prayer; opportunities to repent; offers of mercy; the Bible; the preached gospel; special calls of Providence; special calls of the Spirit; the love of Christ.

2. Coming to himself.

Describe him as he came in sight of his father's mansion; describe the father; contrast in their appearance; faint resemblance of the contrast between the sinner and his heavenly Father; fell on his neck;

what if the son had then turned away and preferred the love of harlots to his father's love. Would not such conduct resemble that of some sinners at the present day? Apply the whole to those present.

VII.

THE STRAIT GATE.

First meeting of the school-year. Remarks about the solemnity of our position. The object of this meeting. Interests of the soul to be sought here.

Various states of mind.

1. Some seem to have no state.

2. Possibly a few may have a great aversion to all religion, and a desire to be left alone to themselves.

3. Some are in a strait between religion and the world. Worldly pleasures, worldly companions, and worldly prospects ever more.

4. Some have a general wish that they may in some way become Christians; but it is a very cold wish.

5. Some came from home expecting here to find the pearl of great price.

6. Some perhaps feel constrained and urged by the Spirit to attend to the subject without delay.

Read Matt. vii. 13–29. To guide you through this strait gate, and into this narrow way, is the object of this meeting. Looking forward forty weeks, what will then be your condition?

Who present wish to be guided into this narrow way? With such I will leave three thoughts.

1. You must not expect others to do that which God

requires of you. "Enter ye." He that is mine is mine for himself.

2. Nothing relating to the soul should be deferred till to-morrow which ought to be done to-day.

3. God is your only strength. Go to him — depend on him — ask of him. Go through Christ.

VIII.

Teachings of the Spirit on the subject of Sin.

Rom. vii. 7–15.

1. Sin is every-where a dreadful evil.

2. The holy law of God, against which sin is committed.

3. The displeasure of God with sin and sinners.

4. The just condemnation of the sinner.

5. The personal application of the guilt of sin to one's self.

6. The application of the condemnation of sin to one's self.

7. A great dread and loathing of sin.

8. A fear of future sin.

9. A fear of continuing to sin through eternity.

10. Despair of strength to avoid sin.

11. Despair of a disposition of heart to avoid sin.

12. A personal acquaintance with the misery of the contest between conviction of duty on the one hand, and no heart to perform it on the other.

13. Perfect helplessness and hopelessness of the sinner's condition. This is one class.

There is another.

1. That there is a Friend of sinners.

2. The need and sufficiency of the cleansing and pardoning blood of Christ.

3. The almighty Arm which can reach the sinner's case.

4. The personal application to one's self.

5. The overwhelming feeling which sometimes fills the soul on the reception of salvation.

6. The faint glimmering of hope in Christ which sometimes enters the soul and continues to grow. Oh, that faint glimmering of hope! how unlike despair!

7. A relying on Christ and Christ alone for strength to forsake sin and consecrate one's self to the service of Christ.

IX.

Seeking an Interest in Christ.

Isaiah lv. 1–3, 6, 7, 8; Matt. vii. 7, 8, 13, 14.

1. If you ever do this you must make up your mind to begin.

2. One time is more favorable than another.

3. The favorable time is known to God.

4. It is not known to us.

5. The dreadful condition of those who have passed and lost the best time.

6. The daily danger of meeting and passing the most favorable time. The present is the most favorable time you will ever meet.

(*a*) Circumstances.

1. You are here.

2. You were led to think of it before you came.

3. You have been invited here.

4. God has called you by his voice.
5. God is now calling you.
(*b*) Your condition.
1. Your depravity.
2. Your sin.
3. Your miserable condition in yourselves.
4. Your dependence on God.
5. The salvation promised by Christ,
6. The necessity of being born again.
7. The office of the Holy Spirit.
8. The conviction of your own conscience.
9. The present thoughts now in your minds.
10. The present moving of the Holy Spirit.
Will you seek now?

X.

Seeking the Lord.

Isaiah i. 1–20.

1. A work of great simplicity.
2. A work of great sincerity.
3. A work alone with God.
4. A salvation for yourselves as you are; not as you are not.
5. Such a salvation as is provided, and not such as is imagined.

XI.

Christ Crucified.

This is an appropriate subject to consider at this time; the Holy Spirit now present. It is adapted to every class among us.

1. God so loved the world.

2. His only begotten Son was equal with the Father.

3. From all eternity Christ had this plan of salvation before his infinite mind.

4. He never turned aside from his work.

5. In the fullness of time he came into this world.

6. His whole temporal life given to this work.

7. As the last scenes approached he kept his eye on this great work.

8. The last interview with his disciples.

9. The garden scene.

10. The scene before his murderers.

11. The scene on the cross.

12. His giving up the ghost.

13. His rising from the dead.

14. His ascension.

15. His being seated at the right hand of God to make intercession for *us*. For whom? Among others for us here.

(*a*) Those who have recently been born again.

(*b*) Those who feel anxious for their souls.

(*c*) Those who desire to be interested more deeply than they are.

(*d*) Those who care not for their doings.

His coming in the clouds of heaven. His farewell to his enemies. His welcome to his followers. Their ascension with him to heaven. The gates of heaven shut. The song in heaven of redeeming love. The mingling of the angelic host. The certainty of the eternal presence of Christ. Oblivion of his enemies.

XII.

Choosing the Lord.

Josh. xxiv. 15; Heb. iii. 7, 8.

1. What to choose between? Belief in Christ or unbelief.

2. Love of forgetting sin or the pleasure of pardoned sin.

3. Worldly pleasure or self-denial for Christ's sake.

4. Strength of Christ — weakness of self.

5. Bearing one's own sins, or having them borne by Christ.

6. Presence of Christ in the closet, or alone without any access to God.

7. Rejoicing in the salvation of souls, or an unhappy feeling in having any one saved.

8. Desiring a revival, or a dread lest there should be one.

9. A pleasure in meeting Christians, or a dread of having any one speak to you.

10. Christ's presence through all this dark world, or a wandering alone.

11. Christ's presence as death approaches, or a dread of death.

12. Christ's presence in the last struggle, or passing alone through the solemn scene.

13. Being received to Abraham's bosom, or lifting up the eyes being in torments.

XIII.

Sovereignty of God.

Luke x. 8–16, 21.

In governing the visible and invisible world; especially in the invisible work of grace in the heart.

1. This doctrine a very solemn subject.
2. Peculiarly suited to excite gratitude.
3. Sovereign work carried on by gradual steps.

Three stages.

(1.) The state of being called.

(2.) The turning state.

(3.) The fixed state, unchangeable.

First state; offers of mercy free. No decree makes it necessary to be lost. Raised to heaven in point of privilege. Children of God invited to labor and pray — the mind led along — they may be saved.

Second state; often known only to God. A final fixing of the soul. A final crisis.

(*a*) Of the believing; they can never be lost. They will have a willing mind in God's service, and they will persevere. God knows who are his. We can only know by striving to make our calling and election sure; by continually striving to enter into the strait gate.

(*b*) The dreadful condition of the wicked. Given over of God. Christians may have no heart to pray. They may do wrong, but it is a providence of God. God in his providence may say, pray not for them. They may neglect to labor for them. Here they may do wrong. But in God's providence he may say, turn from them, and shake off the dust of your feet as a testimony against them.

Third state.

(1.) Becoming more like Christ.

(2.) Approaching nearer to their home with him.

(3.) Receiving more assurances of his love.

(4.) They can never fail of grace — can never be lost.

The wicked.

(1.) Given up of God.

(2.) More and more hardened and senseless.

(3.) Approaching nearer their final doom.

(4.) They will never be saved.

Mistake about the second state.

Sometimes very long and sometimes very short.

Some persons think themselves in the third when they are in the second. It makes them reckless. Seek salvation now.

XIV.

THE NEW SONG.

Rev. v. 9.

Christ and his work for us.

1. He has died for us.
2. He has given us his Spirit.
3. He has adopted us as his own.
4. He has forgiven us all our sins.
5. He has engaged himself, and all he has, in our behalf.
6. He will give us his presence.

7. He will give us his sympathy.

8. He will allow us to partake in all which he has and does.

9. He will never leave us.

10. He will stand by us in death.

11. He will shield us at the judgment day.

12. He will take us home to glory.

13. He will teach us the new song.

14. He will reconcile us to our eternal separation from friends.

XV.

The Wailing of Despair.

Matt. xiii. 47–50.

Like the new song, the wailing will enhance the remembrance of the past, and the truth of the present.

1. Christ's love to them when on earth — that slighted love.

2. His agony and death to save them from their present dreadful state.

3. His calling them, and following them with his entreaties of love.

4. His sending the Holy Spirit to urge them to repentance.

5. His yearnings of compassion over them, as he saw them rushing down to death.

6. The destruction of all excuses. The dreadful thought and feeling, "I could have been saved."

7. The remembrance of all friends in heaven.

8. Of the final separation.

9. Of that eternal banishment. But the present, what is it in the breast?

1. Hatred.

2. Self-condemnation, remorse.

3. Despair.

4. Never to end — never to change.

5. The conviction that the love of God demands this endless punishment.

6. Submission of friends in heaven.

7. The gratitude of those in heaven, as they see the smoke of the torment ascend up, for ever and ever.

XVI.

Interesting Chapter in the History of Paul.

1 Cor. ix. 13–27.

1. The general principle, that ministers should be supported.

2. He did not claim this for himself. He must preach the gospel without reference to the earthly reward.

3. His condescension to all.

4. His fear that he might be a castaway, after all.

5. His striving against the world, that he might not be a castaway.

Instruction to us.

1. What a dreadful thing to be a castaway.

2. Danger of being a castaway.

(1.) To every one. The most established Christian.

(2.) To the lambs of the fold. Those who doubt whether they are Christ's lambs by his converting Spirit, or only by his convicting Spirit. These have cause to fear.

(3.) To those who have no hope, how very great is your danger! I look on you and inquire, Will these have any place in heaven? Shall I meet them? Shall I be there myself?

3. Vast importance of resisting worldly temptation. We think of the sovereign grace of God, and we think right. But the sovereign grace of God includes means. In the efficacy of means, he exhibits his sovereignty. He has no need of means, he could set all aside. To all how important, believers and unbelievers.

(1.) Resist bodily temptation, affectation, love of ease, dread of pain.

(2.) Resist worldly friendships and intimacies.

(3.) Resist temptations of your own heart, dread of being watchful, love of excitement, and of following it.

(4.) Love of approbation of others. Remember Christ's words, Matt. v. 29, 30.

XVII.

The Burden of Sin—Past, Present, and Future.

Ezek. xvi. 1–13; 53–63

1. Convictions of impenitent, only partial.

(1.) No light from Calvary.

(2.) Present sin no great burden.

(3.) Outward reform sufficient.

2. Some hopeful persons are in the dark.

(1.) Dark in hope.

(2.) Dark in view of Christ.

I should love to stop and dwell on Christ. His undying condescension. His unparalleled sufferings. His present glory.

(3.) Dark in view of sin.

3. But not so all.

(1.) The light of Calvary shines.

(2.) In this light what a dreadful burden is sin.

(*a*) What a great sinner I have been.

(*b*) What a great sinner I now am.

(*c*) How I dread future sins; I know I have an Advocate; I can not abuse him.

(*d*) How I long for complete deliverance. Oh, to be holy!

Many a one, on a dying bed, looks to death as the happy deliverance from sin.

XVIII.

Review of the Past.

Deut. xxx. 11–20.

The last Sabbath evening of the term.

1. My responsibility to you, — to God rather for you.

2. My conscious fidelity, and my great unworthiness.

3. Contrast between our first and our last meeting.

(1.) The anticipation; that of myself and you. My work in prospect — your anticipations; to some a privilege, to some a burden.

(2.) Now it is done, it is like death. So death will come.

4. What hath God wrought?

5. How has God been resisted?

6. Death will come upon us like this meeting, — some in readiness; some like the foolish virgins; some without God.

7. You hear my voice for the last time; the last time of Christ's voice.

8. I have set before you life and death.

9. I give you one more invitation, one more entreaty to the impenitent.

10. I exhort all who indulge a hope of salvation.

XIX.

Satan's Grand Temptation.

Gen. ii. 8–17; iii. 1–13.

Thou shalt not surely die.

A very solemn and awful state to be without hope in Christ. A question of infinite importance, How shall I escape?

God is saying, Do this and thou shalt find salvation; neglect, and thou shalt surely die.

The difficulty of embracing true religion.

There are great difficulties. God says you must begin, notwithstanding.

Satan says you can not.

What are these difficulties?

1. The coldness of feeling.
2. The hardness of feeling.
3. The difficulty of thinking.
4. The difficulty of praying.
5. The difficulty of repenting.
6. The difficulty of believing.

With reference to time, God says *now*, or thou shalt surely die. Satan says, Thou shalt not die.

With reference to religion itself.

It is simple, — simplicity of the gospel.

It is direct, — believe and thou shalt be saved.

It humbles self, and magnifies God.

It puts self out of sight, exalts God as all.

It is not of works.

This, an important truth, always brought before the

conscience by the Holy Spirit; always strenuously opposed by Satan. This the grand difficulty.

XX.

Penitence for Sin.

Luke vii. 36–50; xviii. 9–14.

1. Impenitence most unreasonable.

2. Impenitence greatly increases the sinner's guilt.

3. Penitence an easy duty.

4. But penitence is the gift of God. (The fruits of the Spirit.)

5. The penitent feels himself to be the greatest sinner. We could not be penitent and have any other feeling.

(*a*) Because he sees the internal source of his own sin. We can see nothing in the vilest wretch to equal it.

(*b*) He sees the internal aggravating circumstances of his own sin, and he can see nothing in any other one equal to it.

(*c*) His reason or philosophy can never prove, till all hearts are revealed, that he is not what he feels himself to be — the very highest in the scale of sinners.

6. There are all degrees of penitence, from the faintest — scarcely dreamed by the soul itself — to the most overwhelming.

7. Penitence of the penitent is ever increasing.

8. Penitence is greatly increased by an assurance of forgiveness

9. The true penitent will fix his eye on God — an injured God, a forgiving God — more than on self; guilty, polluted self.

XXI.

The Holy Spirit.

John xvi. 7–15; iii. 1–12. Connection of his work with Christ.

1. He is too holy to come to the heart of the sinner only by the cross.

2. Christ must go before, and finish his suffering, atoning work.

3. He must appear before the Godhead and plead his death, and thus send the Spirit. "He ever liveth to make intercession."

4. He teaches about Christ. He, who was as a root out of dry ground, becomes altogether lovely.

The teaching of the Spirit of great importance to every one.

1. Without this there is no possible hope.

2. The Spirit can be grieved away.

3. He comes not at our call.

None will call for him when he is away.

4. We know not when he is present always, but we can see his work; and we can feel that he was here, and has gone, and left his great work, himself unseen.

5. The work of the Spirit is often the gentle whisper. Listen to the faintest whisper.

XXII.

Electing Love of God.

Eph. i. 1–12; ii. 1–10. Electing love, no electing hate.

God elects for heaven — sinners elect themselves for hell.

This a truth of great solemnity, sublimity, and of power.

To many a source of death unto death. This according to a general principle.

1. Some led to neglect the Bible.
2. Some to become infidels.
3. Some to give up seeking religion. To-morrow we die.
4. Some to entertain hard thoughts of God. They look not on God's electing love, but they think of him as electing them to misery. But it has proved a source of life unto many.

1. Some have been led to fear to contend against such a God.
2. Some have been aroused from stupidity by this truth.
3. Some cavilers have been silenced, — have feared to speak and think, and so have stood still and submitted to God.
4. Some have been led to fear to trust to their own future efforts, — have seen their lost and helpless condition.
5. Some have seen the love of God.

6. Some have been aroused from a state of almost despair.

They thought they had sinned away the day of grace, but their thoughts of a day of grace had not been measured by the electing love of God.

7. Some who have thought their case peculiar.

8. Some who have almost ventured to hope in Christ have, by this, been led to trust.

OUTLINES OF ADDRESSES AT MORNING AND EVENING SERVICES.

I.

Respect and Honor of Parents.

Eph. vi. 1–3.

Honor them when they are absent or dead.

1. By pleasing your teacher.
2. Doing what will meet their wishes when absent.
3. By avoiding folly of all kinds.
4. By choosing such companions as your parents would choose for you.
5. By faithfulness in all things.
6. By becoming valuable members of this family.
7. By serving the Lord.

Begin now, is my serious advice.

II.

The Law of God.

Matthew xxii. 35–40.

Two great commandments. The perfections of this law.

1. Its correspondence with eternal right.
2. Its agreement with the holy character of God.
3. Its agreement with human conscience.
4. Its agreement with the glory of God.
5. Its agreement with the happiness of man.

How made known?

Originally by being written on the mind and heart. Rom. i. 18–21; ii. 11–16.

This beautiful law obliterated and darkened by depravity and sin.

Its holy obedience all gone, but not all of its impressions.

The image of God in its holiness gone — all gone; but a remnant of his real image remains in the mind and heart of every one.

The law given us again by a new revelation through Christ, the light of the world.

The Bible is a transcript of God's holy law. The most condensed summary is the Ten Commandments. All who love God, love his holy laws. Those who hate God, hate his holy laws.

Read Psalm cxix. How many times repeated: Thy law — thy precepts — thy word — thy statutes — thy judgments — thy commandments — thy ways.

III.

Reasons for making a public Profession.

Matt. xxviii. 19, 20; Mark xvi. 12; Luke xii. 1–9; Acts ii. 37, 38; xxii. 16.

1. The honor of God demands it. Essential to honoring God *before men.*

2. The authority of God demands it. A great change in the institutions of God since Abraham's day. All religious ceremonies positive. The form not important, but the thing essential. God blesses every form when the doctrine is evangelical. The belief that this is not important can not be remedied in any plan by any degree of piety.

3. Peace of conscience requires it.

4. No one can be for Christ in the protracted neglect of this duty. They must be against him.

5. God will not bless the labors of those who live in this neglect.

6. Whoever lives in the continued neglect of this duty must destroy instead of saving souls.

Objection.

I do not know that I am a Christian. This can not be admitted as an excuse.

IV.

Hatred to Christ.

John xv. 18–27.

1. Universality of this hatred.

2. Manifested by opposition and neglect.

3. The principal channel for pouring forth hatred to the Father. Christ's words, "if ye had known me ye should have known my Father."

4. Hatred for Christ's sake — to God — to his law — to his love — to the disciples of Christ.

5. Exciting cause of hatred — "had not known sin" — comparatively.

6. No excuse left by Christ for sin. Mouth stopped. And why?

(1.) Because Christ bears our sins for us. No pleading weakness, or ignorance, or thoughtlessness, or circumstances. No seeking thus to escape.

(2.) Because Christ is our advocate with the Father.

(3.) Because Christ washes our robes in his blood.

(4.) Because Christ is ready to strengthen us to forsake sin.

(5.) Because Christ will finally present us spotless before the throne (not we ourselves).

7. Hatred to Christ because he removes the excuse for sin.

8. Hatred to Christ without a cause.

9. Hatred to Christ because he is their best friend And why?

(1.) They are enemies to their own souls, and they hate Christ because he loves their souls.

(2.) They seek to destroy their own souls, and they hate Christ because he seeks to save them.

(3.) They love Satan because he unites with them in hating their souls.

(4.) They love Satan because he unites with them in destroying their souls.

10. They hate Christ because of his unspeakable love, amazing condescension, and his glorious work of salvation.

How dreadful is hatred to Christ!

V.

Living to God and living to the World.

Rom. vi. 1–16; xii. 1; 1 Cor. vi. 19, 20; x. 31; Phil. i. 19–23.

Doing our common business for the Lord or against him.

1. With prayer — without prayer.
2. With the feeling, "If the Lord will," — without this feeling.
3. With the impression that this earth is the Lord's and the fullness thereof — and without it.
4. With a connection in our feeling between the commands of God and a perfect standard of doing what we undertake — and without this.
5. With the feeling that eternity is the end of every thing in time — and without this.

VI.

Prayer of Faith.

Praying this prayer for our own family.

What to pray for?

1. That here may abide the manifest presence of God.

2. That every person may be brought under the control of this influence.

3. That every action and every event may be brought under the control of this influence.

4. That all the souls here may be saved.

5. That all doubting souls may be delivered from bondage.

6. That real Christians "may be holy as God is holy."

7. That as a family we may advance in the divine life. This felt in recess meetings — in morning devotions — on the Sabbath — during recreation day.

How shall we seek this spirit of prayer — this prayer of faith?

1. By looking at the subject as an important reality.

2. By living with the solemnities of eternity in our hearts.

3. By giving up our own souls to God.

4. By opening our hearts to receive Jesus Christ.

5. By abiding in Jesus Christ.

6. By following in the footsteps of Jesus Christ.

Finally, let us seek first of all to follow in the footsteps of Jesus Christ — to live as he did — to walk as he walked — to pray as he prayed — to suffer with him, if need be, as he suffered.

VII.

Christian Fellowship.

John x. 11–16; xiv. 20; xvii. 9–11, 20–24.

1. Union together in Christ the most exalted union among created beings.

2. A principle destined to grow.

3. It must grow by nourishment, — not by medicine, but by nourishment enjoyed and relished in the partaking.

This nourishment is, —

1. Sympathy together with Christians through their Head.

2. United worship.

3. United efforts.

4. Choosing the society of Christians. Especially in choosing intimate friends, principle must take the place of feeling.

5. Thanking God, as Paul did, for all their good. 1 Cor. xiii. 4–7.

VIII.

Self-Examination.

Eph. ii. 1–10; 19–22.

Have we evidence of being reconciled to God?

Kind, rather than degree, decisive.

1. A humble and contrite heart. Every iota in the holy life of a Christian casts light on himself, and

sinks him lower in his own view, and gives him new views of himself as a sinner.

2. A believing heart on Jesus Christ.

(1.) As the Saviour.

(2.) As my Saviour.

Every thing sets forth the Saviour — sin, holiness, my sins, my feeble efforts in his service.

3. A subdued spirit.

The *preciousness of being and feeling* subdued under God.

4. Desire for the glory of God in salvation.

5. A subduing of all things in our hearts unto Christ.

Our joys and our sorrows; our hopes and our fears; our present delights and our future prospects.

6. A hungering and thirsting after holiness of heart and life.

Groaning under sin, and longing to be delivered from easily besetting sins; from sins in little things; from sins unseen by others; from sins not esteemed sins by others.

7. A spiritual conscientiousness.

8. An impress of eternity on temporal things.

IX.

Christ the grand Moving Power in Self-denial for Christ's sake.

Book of Hebrews abounds in this motive: iii. 1–6; xii. 1–11; xiii. 12–14.

Applied to giving money.

That we may abound, be steadfast, unmovable, increasing, and advancing — let us look at Christ.

1. A view of what Christ has done alone can give us that love of others which we must have.

2. Having a love of others like Christ's love, we must look at him to feel the worth of their souls.

(1.) Through the light of Christ's agony we get a glimpse of hell.

(2.) Through the light of Christ's agony we get a glimpse of heaven.

3. Looking at Christ's work can give us confidence that we are right.

4. Looking at Christ can give a spiritual interest in our work.

5. Looking to Christ will give us strength to bear poverty — the want of all things.

6. Looking at Christ will make us willing to bear the reproach.

There is a reproach — a reproach that can be felt. This is a trial, the end of which you will not meet in this world. You climb and gain one peak only to discover a new one.

But, 7. Looking to Christ will give us respect to the final reward. Through Christ we can behold the joy set before us — the crown of rejoicing.

X.

Christ's Prayer for his Disciples.

John xvii.

1. The fact. Christ at prayer.

(1.) Who is it? Infinite condescension.

(2.) For whom? Wonderful grace.

2. Pleas used by Christ.

(1.) They were given to him of God the Father.

(2.) Christ had manifested his name to them.

(3.) Their union with God the Father and the Son.

(4.) Christ glorified in them.

3. Particulars of this prayer.

(1.) That they may be kept and not lost. Why shall we not fall as Adam did? Why not fall as the angels did?

(2.) That they may be kept from the evil of the world. When you pray for this, think of Christ's prayer.

(3.) That they may be sanctified through the truth.

(4.) That their joy may be fulfilled.

The glory of salvation unfolded in this prayer.

1. Their union with the Father and the Son.

2. Their like union with each other.

3. Comparison between their relation to Christ and Christ's relation to God: v. 18, 21, 22, 23, 26.

4. Christ, as God, wills in their behalf.

The Godhead vailed, but uncovered at the close of this prayer.

XI.

Feeding the Lambs.

John xxi. 15–23.

1. What is it to feed sheep and lambs?

2. Who are to do this? *All* — the weakest believers.

(1.) This agrees with the whole tenor of the gospel system.

(2.) It agrees with the experience of every new-born soul.

(3.) It agrees with the experience of every returning backslider.

(4.) It agrees with the experience of every advanced Christian.

3. This is a great privilege.

(1.) To deliver immortal beings from eternal death.

(2.) To give them a place with the redeemed.

(3.) Because they are Christ's lambs.

a. His by creation.

b. His by his providence.

c. His by his purchase.

d. His because he is seeking their salvation.

XII.

KILLING THE LAMBS.

Ezekiel xxxiii. 1–9.

Contrast to the command, "Feed my lambs."

How? 1. Neglect of the heart. God looks on the heart of Christians in sending the Holy Spirit.

2. Neglect of prayer.

3. Religious deportment deficient.

4. A worldly deportment suited to draw the heart from God.

The daily deportment a channel through which God bestows or withholds his blessings. Confine to one prominent point — a heedless, trifling, noisy manner.

Specify — rooms — spaceway — domestic work — dining hall.

The sad thought of having destroyed a soul!

1. It is like Satan and not like God.

2. It is acting in opposition to the God whom we love.

3. It is bringing misery upon those whom we love as our own souls.

4. Their blood will be required at our hand.

5. It is in opposition to all the strongest desires of the Christian's heart.

The cause.

1. In the heart.

2. In wrong principles.

3. In deficient self-denial.

Remedy: watch and pray.

XIII.

First Meeting of a Term.

2 Peter i.

The solemnity of our present position.

My responsibility in this meeting.

Your responsibility.

Your duty as Christians.

Seek to know that you are not deceived.

Do this by proving yourselves to be Christians.

1. Before God; 2. To yourself; 3. To others.

This the natural order — this the order of importance.

I shall reverse the order.

To others.

How? 1. By general manner.

2. Religious aspect. (1.) Meetings; (2.) Sabbath; (3.) Bible lesson; (4.) Religious conversation.

3. Serious and stable character.

4. Consistent character.

5. Benevolent character — not selfish.

6. Self-denial.

7. Resisting temptation.

To yourselves.

1. By having a conscience void of offense.

2. By feeling your own unworthiness.

(1.) To be called a Christian.

(2.) To be allowed to be faithful.

3. Labor for Christ.

4. Suffer for Christ.

5. Feel a confidence in God — an unspeakable trust.

6. Have faith in Christ.

Before God.

God knows; and yet say to him, "Thou knowest all things, thou knowest that I love thee."

XIV.

The Christian Hope

Heb. xii. 1–24.

To be left to doubt is one of the greatest chastenings of a young Christian.

Reasons why some are thus left — to try them.

1. To make them solemn.

2. To make them humble.

3. To make them love the gospel for its own sake. *The* hope — instead of my hope — should often fill the mind.

4. To prepare them to entertain and give a consistent and uniform reason for the hope within them.

5. To prepare them to be stable Christians; not changeable.

6. To prepare them to enter on a Christian life as a subject of trial rather than of enjoyment — of tribulation — patience.

7. To prepare them to labor for the salvation of others.

8. To prepare them to act in obedience to the commands of Christ rather than according to their own present feelings.

XV.

Prayer of Faith for the Holy Spirit.

Luke xi. 1–13.

1. What is prayer? Social or public prayer? Secret prayer?

One is like dwelling in the outer court; the other like entering the inner temple. None enter the inner temple who are not found in the outer court.

2. Objects of prayer: — Every want; every grief; every anxiety; every temptation; every friend and every foe.

But prayer for spiritual blessings for ourselves and others is the essence of prayer.

In what do spiritual blessings consist?

In the gift of the Holy Spirit. Nothing is given us but by the Holy Ghost. He is the messenger. He takes of the things of Christ and gives them unto us.

3. What is a prayer of faith?

General faith implies confidence — trust — reliance — belief in God — in Christ.

In special faith the heart filled with great truths. The great atonement by Christ; the infinite; the eternal condition in eternity; the helpless condition of men; the fullness of salvation; the power of the Holy Ghost; the promises of the Holy Ghost.

4. There are special calls for a special prayer of faith.

The disciples at Jerusalem; providential circumstances; our condition in this Seminary every year; this year.

XVI.

Salvation of those who have sinned against great light.

Ezekiel xxxvi. 1–38.

1. Sinning against better knowledge a great dishonor to God.

2. Such are miserable in their sins. In their miserable state they sin the more.

3. God has pity on them.

4. It is for his own mercies' sake.

5. God's name greatly glorified in the salvation of such sinners.

6. An inward, not an outward, change simply.

7. An outward change, also.

8. Such pardoned sinners will loathe and abhor themselves.

9. They are exhorted to be ashamed and confounded.

10. When such are forgiven, others will know that it is the work of God.

11. God will be inquired of to do it.

XVII.

Wisdom.

Prov. ii.

1. Be wise in diligence.
2. In self-control.
3. In spending your time.
4. In choice of companions.
5. In conversation.
6. In exercising a benevolent disposition.
7. In seeking the glory of God, rather than your own praise.
8. In seeking for the will of God, rather than your own will.
9. In trusting in God rather than in yourself.
10. In depending on Christ's atoning blood for free pardon.
11. In seeking for heaven rather than earth.
12. In seeking that others may be blessed, instead of thinking of yourself.

XVIII.

The great Choice.

Joshua xxv. 14–27.

A very important subject for you to consider at this time, and to attend to without delay.

1. Because the subject of choice is infinitely greater than any other. It is a choice between heaven and hell. What is this? Think of hell. The light of heaven is shut out from some, and hell opens and shoots forth some glimmerings of its dreadful fires. Think of its intense torments — of its eternal damnation!

2. Because all will not be saved.

3. Because no impenitent sinner can have any promise of being among the saved.

4. Because the heart is deceitful above all things, and can not be trusted.

5. Because you are claimed and sought after by the inhabitants of the two worlds.

6. Because your salvation is entirely dependent on the Holy Spirit.

7. Because the Holy Spirit has special seasons for this special work in the heart.

8. Because the Spirit can be grieved.

9. Because individuals have a special call to repent.

10. Because God is now present here by his Holy Spirit, and may, for aught I know, and for aught you know, be giving you this special call.

11. Because there is great danger of not believing

the truth taught you by the Holy Spirit, but of believing a lie which is taught by Satan.

12. Because God has no pleasure in the death of the wicked.

13. Because there is joy in heaven over one sinner that repenteth.

XIX.

Praying Always.

1. Pray for yourselves; for yourself as an individual. Connect your prayer with your duty in the great work of converting the world. What does God require of you, and what should you be to do it?

2. Pray for the conversion of souls. Connect their conversion with their future work in the conversion of the world.

3. Pray for the continued prevalence of religion in our family. Look at the example of Paul in this respect. What large blessings he sought. At the example of Jesus Christ. Connect this with the conversion of the world. God often connects great results with small things done in sincerity and faith.

4. Pray directly for the conversion of the world: —

1. Dwell on the promises that this world shall be converted. Read them. Pray over them.

Pray that the fulfillment of these promises may be hastened. Dwell on the infinite importance that they should be hastened. Think of the multitudes who perish every year, and will continue to perish till the promises are fulfilled. What will the fulfillment be to them when it comes? Think of the truth, that it can be hastened by prayer, and that it can be delayed by unbelief.

2. Pray for the prevalence of a missionary spirit. Pray that all who are converted may be converted to the missionary work, with a missionary spirit. How many reasons why it should be so. It was so with Paul. Who that has known the terrors of the law or the love of Christ can but have a missionary spirit?

3. Pray that the Spirit of God may be poured out on all Christians, and, by the light that shines roundabout them, they may see the importance of the missionary work.

4. Pray for the success of missionary operations.

5. Pray for a blessing on missionary societies; American Board, and other societies.

6. Pray for missionaries themselves, mentioning them by name.

7. Pray for particular stations.

8. Pray for all those who have gone from this Seminary, enumerating each, and the fields where they are laboring. Write their names.

9. Pray for all who are laboring at home in an eminent degree, either personally or by their money.

10. Pray for a universal spirit of liberality, and a universal spirit of prayer.

XX.

Regeneration.

John iii. 1–11.

1. An entire change.
(1.) Not of the mind.
(2.) But of the religious character.
2. The figures new birth — raising from the dead.
3. As great as any miracle.
4. Not very obvious always to the individual, but to God.
5. Manifestations of increase of grace like the growth of an infant.
6. A work beyond the scrutiny of man.
7. The circumstances not to be calculated upon, not to be predicted.
8. A revival not to be talked about or calculated upon when in progress.
9. This pre-eminently the work of God.
10. The crowning work of Jesus Christ.
11. Prayer, how appropriate; how full of wisdom and goodness its appointment.

XXI.

Sin without Excuse before the Cross of Christ.

1. Its universality. By a view of the cross it becomes an individual subject.

2. General confession. At the cross the contrite heart needs something more.

3. A general desire to become a Christian often gives a feeling of complacency, and a cloak for sins. At the cross this desire is lost sight of.

4. A discouraged feeling about becoming a Christian is a cloak for sin.

5. Excuses for neglecting to seek salvation.

(1.) It will do no good for me to try.

(2.) I would try if I knew I should succeed.

(3.) I have once had a false hope, and now I want a good one, or none.

(4.) What will others think of me?

XXII.

Entering God's Vineyard.

Matt. xx. 1–16.

1. God has a vineyard.

2. It is a great privilege to be called into it.

3. He rewards.

4. The reward gratuitous.

5. Those called into the vineyard often most unworthy.

6. At a late period, sometimes.

(1.) Late in age.

(2.) Late in having refused invitations.

7. Motives to enter the vineyard. Not an idle service.

8. Encouragement to all to ask for a place.

9. Encouragement to hope against hope.

Necessity of a spirit of entire consecration to God, as is illustrated in the life of Abraham.

XXIII.

God's Mercy.

Psalm cxxxvi.

The great principle in the divine economy. "His mercy endureth for ever."

Vs. 1–3. Leading attributes in God's revealed character calling for praise and thanksgiving.

4–9. Grand cause for all the works of God in creation and providence.

10–20. Grand reason for his judgments and the exhibitions of his wrath.

21–24. Reasons for giving to some and withholding from others.

25. Temporal blessings.

26. General thanksgiving to God.

1. We can see why God punishes. To lead others to repentance.

2. We can see why he forbears. To lead to repentance.

3. In the bestowment of temporal blessings God has a higher design than immediate good.

4. The grand cause of salvation to any.

Two impressions on my mind — one dark the other full of light.

As a great whole the punishment of the wicked

seems wise and good — most for the glory of God; most for the glorious happiness of the created universe. With this view we can join in thanksgiving for his judgments.

But looking at individuals, our hearts are filled with anguish and our feeble minds clouded with mystery. We may sympathize with Christ in his weeping over Jerusalem. "Why was I made to hear thy voice?" Even so, Father, for so it seemed good in thy sight.

Christians should be made solemn, penitent, and prayerful.

They should bear their own sins and the condition of sinners on their hearts as they enter the holy place, and lay them on the head of the Lamb of God. Sinners should tremble lest they should be left, and strive to make their calling and election sure.

I shall never read this verse again without recalling the impressive manner in which it was spoken just one week ago by Miss Washburn; how she repeated, "for ever, for ever, for ever;" adding, "who can tell what that means?" Even judgments are to show that his mercy endureth for ever.

XXIV.

Faith of Abel.

Heb. xi. 4; Gen. iv. 2–5; 1 John v. 12.

1. First recorded instance of a sacrifice.
2. Institution of sacrifices a wonderful event.
3. Describe the reason.

4. Abel's penitence and Abel's faith in Christ.

5. Abel's sudden admission into the presence of Christ.

6. Abel being dead yet speaketh. The dead in Christ send a voice after them.

1. He speaks to the impenitent. He was penitent.

2. He speaks to the unbelieving. He had faith in Christ.

3. He speaks to the self-righteous. He was clothed in Christ's righteousness.

4. He speaks to those who depend on a religion which does not purify the life. His works were righteous.

5. He speaks to those who neglect great light.

6. He speaks encouragement to the desponding.

7. He magnifies the grace of God.

8. He speaks in a voice of praise and glory to God. He has commenced the new song.

9. Joy among the angels when he entered heaven. "Glory to God in the highest."

10. His joy over every repenting sinner.

11. His joy at every new meeting of a redeemed and sanctified soul.

XXV.

Glorying in Infirmities.

Not in sins, but in infirmities.

1. Our greatest excellences have, by their side, some humiliating fault. This is then the subject of glory through our excellences.

2. Christ often employs the weakest instruments. We may be encouraged by this.

3. There is often a needful thorn. Needful to open the way for communications of glory; for blessed success in our work.

4. Our prayers are sometimes not answered, that we may desire more than we can ask or think. How much better to have the thorn and grace than to have no thorn and no grace.

5. The thorn often grows in our own character. This gives it its sharpness.

6. There is a mystery in being reconciled to our own mistakes and missteps, and yet groaning to be delivered from all sin; a mystery known only to the heart of the believer.

Effects of glorying in infirmity.

1. Our guilt magnifies the grace of God.

2. Our corruption magnifies the power of the Spirit on our hearts.

3. Our weakness magnifies the strength of Christ.

4. Our unworthiness magnifies the condescension of Christ.

5. A conviction of our unfitness to receive the blessing sought overwhelms us with gratitude when the blessing comes.

XXVI.

Taking no thought for the morrow.

Matt. vi. 25–34.

1. Religion, in general, is a present subject; not future nor past.

2. Duty is present.
3. Repentance.
4. Faith.

Advantages of this course.

1. Persons can sustain what is laid upon them.
2. They can do the most trying things. Abraham.
3. They can bear the greatest burdens.
4. They can venture to go forward.

XXVII.

Christ the Light of the World.

John i. 4–9 ; iii. 19–21.

Human depravity and wickedness are the darkness of the world.

1. Christ is the grand theme of the Bible.
2. The grand subject presented to the heart by the Holy Spirit.
3. The grand object of opposition by the powers of darkness and by wicked men.
4. Christ is every thing to us ; we live in him ; for him ; to him.

FASTING.

I.

Observance of the Day.

Fasting has always been observed by eminent Christians. Christ spoke of it, as a matter of course, as an established thing — "when ye fast." We should fast in view of our sins and in view of our necessities. There should be no compulsion in reference to the observance of the day; but we shall wish to have our house entirely quiet; let the wheels of business stop, and, as it were, step into eternity and spend the day. I hope the impenitent will think how they are slighting the offers of mercy.

To spend time in religious services, is like bringing the alabaster box and pouring it on the Saviour's head. We should give the best of this day to religion. If it is asked, Why is this alabaster box broken? — the answer is, From love to the Saviour. Spending time purely for religion, is more nearly like the service of heaven than any thing else. Let us seek to spend the day so as to have a realization of eternity. Depart far out of the world, and may you come back profited.

II.

What is Fasting?

Fasting — *literally* to abstain from food; extended to mean to abstain from all worldly pleasures or worldly gratifications — society, reading, study, walking, riding, writing letters, worldly musings. *Spiritually* — to afflict the soul by bringing painful subjects before the mind.

Painful subjects.

1. How many sins I have committed.
2. How unfit I am now for the Lord's work.
3. The dreadful world of misery.
4. The many who have gone there, the painful emotions in view of it.
5. The fear that I may go there and fail at last.
6. The danger in which others now stand. The hazard of every one without hope. The danger of deathbed repentance — the danger of delay — the painful feeling of seeing an impenitent sinner appear happy. The ignorant, who have none to teach them, parents nor teachers; their danger — the heathen — every individual and their danger.
7. The duties I have neglected, the wrong examples I have set; the dishonor I have cast on God; the souls I have led away from God.
8. The low state of religion — the low standard of duty.
9. Look at institutions of learning.

III.

Fast for Colleges.

We met at the usual time for devotions. Miss Lyon said there were two objects she wished us to pray for to-day — the outpouring of the Holy Spirit in this family, and upon literary institutions. In praying for this family, pray especially for the impenitent. Look at the encouraging side in doing this. She then read 2 Chron. xx. 20, also Luke v., the miraculous draught of fishes. How many of these dear teachers and pupils would say, We have toiled all the night, and taken nothing. There are a few in the dear senior class who have no hope. Can they not say they have toiled all the day, and all the night too, and taken nothing? Will they not let down their nets to-day, and let us all, yes, every one, let down our nets in their behalf? Then she turned to the middle class, and asked the same of them, and of the junior class, who are yet impenitent. Are you willing to toil on month after month as you have done, and take nothing? Let down your nets to-day, and let us all let them down, and see if we have not a great blessing.

At half past two P. M. all were invited to a meeting in the Seminary Hall. (For the subject of remarks, see following section.)

IV.

Descent of the Holy Spirit on Literary Institutions.

Acts ii. 12–21; Joel ii. 12–32; Isaiah xliv. 1–18; lix. 19–21.

1. The duty of praying for the descent of the Holy Spirit on literary institutions.

(1.) Colleges.

(2.) Theological seminaries.

(3.) Preparatory institutions.

(4.) Female schools.

(5.) Common schools.

(6.) Schools for children.

2. Duty of all teachers to make this an express object. Always keep it in mind. God has laid this on you.

(1.) In preparing to be teachers.

(2.) In seeking a place to teach.

(3.) In the immediate anticipation of a definite school.

(4.) As you commence teaching.

(5.) As you go on from day to day and from week to week. You may inquire what you shall do. "We know not what to do." 2 Chron. xx. 12. "But our eyes are on thee." I should not dare to try to tell you very definitely what to do. But feel that you must do something, and look to God to teach you what it is.

3. Encouragement to labor.

(1.) Promises of God to youth.

(2.) Promises of God to faithful instruction.

(3.) Promises to prayers.

(4.) Past goodness of God.

Did a teacher ever enter on the work of teaching as a work for the Lord, looking by prayer and faith for the conversion of their pupils, who was not blessed?

Favorable circumstances.

1. Teachers to unite with parents for the conversion of their children.

2. Their common work would be an aid. Train the mind, cultivate the conscience, self-control, system, etc.

3. The newness of the acquaintance, and the newness of their situation.

4. The shortness of the connection.

5. The approaching separation.

Who will venture to defer repentance to a better season?

DETACHED SAYINGS.

Do not yield to inclination instead of judgment in diet, exercise, bathing, rising, etc. Attend to all these if you would have religious interest uniform.

Confide in the judgment of your mothers. It will give your mothers great happiness to have you confide all to them, and it is the safer way for you. If your mother is in doubt in reference to a ride, walk, or a correspondence, your duty is certain.

What is duty is duty, though ever so small.

Seek to understand propriety in your intercourse with gentlemen. It is important to have this knowledge at the right time, that you may do nothing that will be a matter of regret to you.

Form little rules for the improvement of character, but do not speak of them.

Take just as good care of little things as large ones. The young lady who will leave a spoon out of place, or drop a dipper where she may chance to use it, can hardly expect to have a great deal committed to her.

Character may be compared to a piece of embroidery, which is all accomplished stitch by stitch.

So live that it will be pleasant for others to think of you when you are dead.

When curses are denounced upon children for parents' sake, it is upon wicked children for wicked parents' sake.

Do not allow pride to make you silent. Some think they can say nothing worth saying. Probably none of us can; but if communing together is appointed as a means of good, we should not neglect it.

Be careful in regard to what you do yourself, and very charitable to others.

Winter is the seed-time of health. Take much exercise in the cold season, if you would be well in summer.

It is as easy to improve five talents as one.

None have more responsibility than others. Teachers have no more than scholars, except comparatively. Absolutely considered in reference to God, all are alike responsible.

If any one thinks he has no responsibilities, it is because he has not sought them out.

One great thing to be gained in an education, is to be able to possess comforts and privileges without becoming selfish.

Decide whether you will be selfish or benevolent characters.

Form such a character in this life as you will wish to possess through eternity.

Seek to be always in such a state of mind, and to so spend each day, that you will be prepared for afflictive intelligence, and even for death itself.

A sense of eternal things constantly upon the mind is calculated to make one uniformly cheerful and happy.

If we do not resolve to act at once when we are interested, the impression will react upon the mind, and wear away its sensitiveness.

Never read a book without first praying over it.

It is better to govern by conscience and judgment than by fear, but better to govern by fear than not at all.

You all possess great power of influencing others, and I am afraid that some of you are weaving webs of sloth, worldliness, or thoughtlessness which you are throwing around your companions.

Poor persons often speak disparagingly of the rich Christian. If they knew all his trials, they would spend the time thus occupied in praying for him.

Remember, there is no kindness you can show a poor person like helping him to do for himself to the extent of his ability.

If we can not yield our will in little things, God will almost certainly give us greater trials. He may not do it at once, but he will not forget that his child needs more discipline, and he will take his own time for giving it.

It is not possible for a person to be thoroughly imbued with a missionary spirit who is not benevolent in other respects.

Good table manners are to be especially sought for in such a family as ours, where, among so many, there is danger of degeneracy. It is said, and I think justly, that a lady is known by her table manners.

In the review of a study at the examination, you will often find that some pages of the book were not well learned when you first went over it. As this troubles you, remember that at the judgment misimproved days will thus come up.

If you have the care of only one little child, never, for a moment, think that you have not a great work. If that child is spared to grow up, it may be that you will influence thousands through him. If he is early taken away, be happy in the thought that you have helped prepare a child for heaven. And we can not know but the child in heaven does more for this world than the most devoted Christian minister spared to see his three-score and ten years on earth.

Ask for a life of growth in all that is good, but do not ask for a life of ease. In asking this you may ask for eternal misery.

Little faith, few works, and a little treasure in heaven, go together.

Taste should be made a subject of practical education. Those articles of dress that are in the best taste do not change as much from year to year as others.

I am always afraid of the influence of those ladies whose principal subject of conversation is plainness in dress. They are very likely to go to the opposite extreme. Self-respect is acquired and retained by some attention to dress. I have only a few brief rules to give you on this subject, and may never speak to you of it again. Never be singular in your dress, but endeavor to dress so as not to be noticed. Never impress people as being fond of dress. Purchase good articles when you purchase any, and seek to use them to the best advantage. I have no idea that Christ was negligent of his dress. His garment was one counted worthy of casting lots upon

Act from principle in regard to going to church. Then you will do right, be it hot or cold, wet or dry. You probably know very little how much your vacant seat in church on the Sabbath affects your pastor. I am sure that it will always do the man of God good to see you regularly in your place in the house of worship, with the interested countenance which always goes with the interested heart.

Seek for yourself a place where the flame of selfishness will not be fanned.

I love to live for you, my dear children; but when I think of myself alone, I want to go home.

Never plead native character as an excuse for your faults. The Bible gives no such excuse.

A good Christian hope will not grow dimmer and dimmer like the taper, but, like the rising sun, brighter and brighter.

Why are some persons in a hurry? Simply on account of slothfulness.

None can be honest to God who are not honest to man.

There is a definite time for every thing. If it is not done at its time, a place can never be found for it without displacing something else. If an hour is lost, it is never regained. We may crowd its duties into other hours, but the day is worth as much less as that hour's value, and even more. This is true of the whole of life.

Bring your strongest intellectual powers into action when you look at the way of salvation.

Many ladies are made most miserable by trying to be fashionable, because they have no character.

The cultivation of the ornamental branches without a thorough education, is like trying to polish cork or sponge; but with that it is the burnishing of the finest gold.

Follow judgment rather than impulse. Of all the leading-strings in the world, the last to follow should be fancy.

We can compare ourselves profitably with others sometimes, and we should be careful not to lose what we thus gain. From the wise, we may learn to be wise; from the impatient, learn to be patient; from the unreasonable, learn the undesirableness of such a course.

Always remember that there is no possible making up of lost time.

There is a deficiency of grasp of mind if you do not think; a deficiency of moral power if you do not care. Want of business habits in ladies consumes their time, their hearts, and gives them much perplexity.

All the sins of the Christian will be remembered in judgment to show the exceeding love of Christ in their forgiveness.

In estimating our obligations we must look at our means, our blessings, and our light. We must look at the wants of a world, — the door open, — and then ask what God requires. Human laws tell us so exactly what to do, there is no room for faith. The Bible is a rule of duty, but leaves room for faith. There are general principles, like great pillars, on which we stand and study our duty.

Do not wait for solicitors to ask for your missionary contributions. Lay aside a portion as for a sacred purpose, and carry it if it is not asked for.

The benevolence of the Jews was, to an extent, expended on their ceremonies. God seemed to say to them, You are not strong enough to convert the world.

No missionary can give up as much as Christ did when he came to this world. We have none of us such a Father's house to leave.

Those obtain the greatest happiness who seek it indirectly by promoting the happiness of others.

Our greatest happiness is derived from our interest in and labor for others. The Christian's greatest joy or sorrow is in regard to others.

Treasure up hints; they may prove the seed of principles.

Wealth and extravagance have no necessary connection.

I have been asked if it would not be well for our young ladies to give an example of economy, and throw their influence in favor of it by pledging themselves to wear certain articles of dress. (There were societies of ninepenny calico then talked of.) I would not like to have you do any thing of this kind. I do not wish you to be singular in your dress. Your time is too precious to be given to such an object. Neither do I think it best for you to confine yourselves to the cheapest articles of dress. It is not economy to do this. Nor do I believe that you will thus accomplish the greatest good.

There is a defect in our present system of education. Knowledge of books increases faster than knowledge of character.

There were more strong characters fifty years ago than now, because knowledge and reflection were better balanced.

The body and the mind each strive for the mastery. The body is of the earth. The mind ranges in eternity. The mind should not sit down and wash the body's feet. The master should have the master's place. Take an illustration. In the morning the mind says, It is time to rise. The body says, It is cold. The mind listens to the body. Servitude and degradation follow. When you know it is time to rise, do it at once. And will you remember it all your lives, and how I stood here and asked you to do it?

Young ladies honor or dishonor parents in every thing they do. Their parents are judged by what they are.

I have often conceived very high respect, and even affection, for the parents of my pupils, before meeting those parents. This has been given me by their faithful daughters.

Parents are often more grieved by the dishonor shown them by their advanced children, than by the disobedience of little children.

Economy for the sake of giving is never mean, but noble.

Many persons are poor not because they have not enough, but because they do not know how to use what they have.

I do not expect to ever want while I have so many grateful pupils.

If I were to educate a young lady to fill the highest post, as far as intellect, wealth, and station were concerned, I would say, she should be strictly economical; repair and mend her dresses rather than give them to the poor, and thus be able to give money that will flow through the world.

Makers of fashion are not usually educated persons. Always give the throne to conscience.

The frequent Sabbath headaches probably arise from change of employment; but we may so rise above them as to be found in church.

It is important for young ladies to decide early in the school year, whether or not they can be cheerful and contented. Homesick people I do not place very high in the scale of character.

Take care of your spelling, writing, reading, and singing.

Humility consists not so much in thinking meanly of one's self, as in feeling one's dependence on a higher power for success. There is no better time for the exercise of humility than when we succeed. The feeling is, Oh! how unworthy I am to be able to succeed.

We ought to appear benevolent, as well as to be really so. This is the reason I think it best to have our missionary contributions in the form of subscriptions.

Do not break a post-office law to save a ninepence or a quarter of a dollar. There is a kind of reverence in keeping law, though it be too strict.

Acquire the habit of accounting for time as well as money. Yet avoid appearing too economical of time; as when taking a book or paper into company. A lady should be so educated that she can go as a missionary at a fortnight's notice.

The feeling which leads us to say, I may do what others may not; my case is peculiar, — prevents a vast amount of good in families, communities, and the world.

Cultivate foresight, and a habit of looking on the bright side. Nothing except a good conscience contributes more to an habitual cheerfulness than this habit.

Cherish such a frame of mind as to be continually prepared for great and sudden events.

In reading for devotion, it is more profitable to read a few verses. Read a little, and let the truths fall into your mind. Receive them just as they drop, as it were, voluntarily into the mind, and see if some thought does not seem most precious. Many make a great mistake in making too great an effort to feel. You should not make much effort. Keep the mind on the passage, without wandering. This is very important. If you have one thought peculiarly precious, just think why you have it: because you have your mind on the Bible. Perhaps these precious thoughts will be some of the same you will have in heaven.

The commands of God in the first ages are definite and simple, like those of a parent to young children. Little children can not infer their duties from general commands, but older ones can judge of parents' wishes from definite commands given to the younger. This renders their obedience higher, nobler, more gratifying to parents than if exact rules were given. In the same manner God leads us, his elder children, to infer our duty from directions given to the younger — those living in earlier ages.

All are not required to act in relation to the same laws. Angels are not called upon to obey their parents, for they have no parents. Every command must be obeyed so far as individuals are called to act in relation to it.

If the ceremonial law and moral law had been mingled and delivered together, there would have been ground for caviling at the latter. But it does not say, "Thou shalt have no other gods before me," and then say, "Thou shalt not seethe a kid in his mother's milk."

The Bible was silent on the subject of keeping the Sabbath many hundred years, in several instances, yet when alluded to it is just as if it were binding.

The Bible has no favorite duties, no favorite laws. The stress the Bible lays upon subjects is proportioned to their importance.

God is glorified by having his plans accomplished. When man's plans are accomplished it proves his wisdom and skill. Just so with God. One way of honoring God is by increasing the happiness of ourselves and friends. Every time we diminish happiness, we dishonor him. When we appear unhappy and dejected, we imply that he made us to be unhappy.

A wish to be remembered after we are dead is not wrong, not pride, unless excessive. The Bible presents this as a motive for action.

More than nine tenths of the suffering we endure is because those around us do not show that regard for us which we think they ought to.

Most wonderful and comprehensive are God's laws. The reason that the ten commandments are given in so little space, is because the willing-hearted understand easily. They understand duty by the general spirit of the Bible; *e. g.*, The spirit of the fifth commandment is, that we observe all *relative* duties.

If you have an excellent father, you ought to respect

him, and so ought every one in the neighborhood; but you have his parental character to respect, too. Even if a child have a wicked, degraded, drunken father, yet he must pay respect to that father as he does to no other person.

The animal creation are not moral agents. They do not design to do things right or wrong, more than the plants that grow out of the ground.

It is one thing to approve, and another to love; one thing to disapprove, and another to hate. Much of our unhappiness arises from loving what we most disapprove.

Settle some great principles of duty for life. All who have ever attained to any great degree of perfection have had certain rules by which to abide. Doubtful cases cause us much trouble. In these refer to your general rule.

The violation of the seventh commandment may and ought to be examined as a general subject, but beware of learning particulars.

Choose the society of such gentlemen as will converse without even once seeming to think that you are a lady.

What course should be taken with children who make inquiries on the subject of births? The mother is the proper person to answer such inquiries. Let her tell them no strange stories, but speak with simplicity, never without sufficient cause, and never in a way to excite further curiosity. She should lead them to feel that they should not speak of the subject, unless to her; that she will talk to them about it when proper, and meanwhile they should be willing to be ignorant.

It is easier to judge without reason than to stop and think.

It is a divine requirement to "take fast hold of instruction." This implies something more than to sit still and merely receive what is brought to our minds. You must *seek* for knowledge, for be assured the heavenly stranger will not force herself into your possession.

A conscience void of offense is the best commentator.

The keeping of the first table of the law is expressed in one word, — worship. One command gives us the object of worship, another the manner of worship, and another, still, the time of worship.

Always treat your room-mates and intimate friends politely.

Always be in haste, but never in a hurry.

Accustom yourself to practice self-denial when it will promote the happiness of others.

Acquire knowledge that you may do good.

Act from principle rather than from feeling.

Always conduct as if your parents were visibly present.

Avoid undue excitement on trivial occasions.

At the close of each day carefully review your conduct.

A time for every thing, and every thing at its time.

Avoid unpleasant looks.

Avoid smiling in meeting, and exchanging looks with an acquaintance.

Avoid loud talking in the streets.

Avoid doing such things as are suited to excite attention.

Be punctual to all appointments.

Be sincere in your professions of friendship.

Cultivate a pleasant countenance.

Endeavor to eradicate prejudice.

Endeavor to acquire that discipline which will enable you to judge correctly of yourself.

Endeavor to improve in conversation.

Endeavor to impart some knowledge of the Bible to some one younger than yourself every week.

Endeavor to gain a thorough knowledge of domestic duties by practice.

Exhibit such an example in your dress, conversation, and temper, as will be worthy of imitation.

Get good and do good.

In every thing you undertake, have some definite object in view.

Investigate every subject with which you would become acquainted, until you understand it.

Learn to bear disappointments cheerfully.

Never call on an individual unless you have a prospect of doing or receiving good.

Never make calls on the Sabbath unless duty requires.

Never speak unless you have something to say, and always stop when you are done.

Never laugh immoderately.

Never smile at the infirmities of others.

Never manifest any peculiar emotion at the looks or appearance of a stranger.

Never be a minute too late.

Never look behind you, or gaze idly at any person in the streets.

Never make sport of an intoxicated or an insane person.

Observe all the rules of politeness at home which you would were you situated among strangers.

Spend time not only profitably, but most profitably.

Study the Bible so much that every week you can perceive you are increasing in knowledge of the sacred Scriptures.

The intellectual miser is an object of contempt.

What ought to be done can be done.

To Teachers.

Never engage to teach where you can not give religious instruction.

Say to scholars, "You must not do this because it is *improper*," not "because you are *scholars*." Whispering, for instance, is always impolite.

A teacher should be careful not to appeal to herself. Let your actions speak.

To improve perception, present objects before the school, and ask definite questions; *e. g.*, "My watch and the bell, do they shine alike?"—referring not to color, but to luster.

Make the dull ones think once a day; make their eyes sparkle once a day.

Make a scholar *decide* as to matters of perception. A book of animals is useful. Compare not the whole animal, but one part.

Avoid giving extra lessons for punishment. You certainly would not make a boy get a lesson for telling a lie.

Never threaten scholars when you punish. If the culprit says, "I didn't know that I should be punished," reply, "I did not expect you would know it; but did you not know it was *wrong?* If not, I will not punish you."

I would not dare say, "Those who have whispered may rise," but, "All may rise. Those who have *not whispered* may sit down."

Always treat parents and former teachers with respect.

Aim to make every lesson interesting.

Avoid having favorites in school.

Ask a scholar to do what you desire in such a manner as you would ask a favor of a companion.

Be willing to devote your whole time to your school, and be willing to make the best use of it.

Convince the scholars that you are their friend.

Do not forbid play as a punishment, but rather forbid study.

Do not frequently mention particular faults.

Encourage the diffident, and humble the forward.

If you have a dull scholar, endeavor to gain his attention, even to the neglect of some others.

Let your affection be manifested in conduct rather than in words.

Let your punishments be such as will affect the mind rather than the body.

Let your punishments be such as to deprive your pupils of some real privilege.

Let the certainty, not the severity, of your punishments inspire dread.

Never make the study of the Bible a punishment.

Never threaten unless you can execute.

Never attempt to correct more than one fault at a time.

Never cherish in your scholars an immoderate ambition.

Never magnify follies and failings.

Never compare one child with another.

Never allow yourself to speak in a fretful, angry tone.

Never make unnecessary remarks upon families.

Never be in haste to believe a pupil has done wrong.

Never make contemptuous remarks upon scholars.

Study every lesson before you give it to be learned.

Teach children to bear disappointments with cheerfulness.

Treat a retiring child with peculiar kindness.

Treat a forward child with apparent indifference.

When children have been accustomed to bad habits, it is better to keep a record of what is right than of what is wrong.

THE END.

www.ingramcontent.com/pod-product-compliance
Lightning Source LLC
LaVergne TN
LVHW020211110826
845151LV00003B/678

* 9 7 8 1 4 2 5 5 3 4 4 9 3 *